This book is dedicated to you,
dear reader.
I'm delighted you want to discover more about
what it means to walk by faith.
I pray you'll discover insights and truths
based on God's Word that will help you walk
hand-in-hand with Jesus.

Acknowledgments

In my experience as a writer it's not often that a publishing company believes so much in an author that they wrap their arms around your work, encourage you while you're writing, and help sustain you as you market your work. I'm blessed to be working with the wonderful people at Harvest House Publishers. The president, Bob Hawkins, and the entire staff with whom I've worked have been nothing but tender when I've been corrected, wise in their decisions, careful to deliver the Word of God accurately, zealous in seeking suggested outlets to market the works, sincere in their dedication to produce a quality product, innovative in their strategic plan for the books—and all this is done with godly integrity.

If I begin to name names I would be hurt if I accidently left anyone out, so I won't do that. There is someone I must name because he isn't a Harvest House employee, and that's my editor Thomas Womack. Thomas, thank you for reading my ideas and material and organizing them into a meaningful and logical progression so people can be helped.

I'd also like to thank David Van Diest, the best literary agent in the world.

A word of thanks to my son, who helped teach me how to walk in faith. His words to me were, "If you pray, Mama, why worry?" In other words, "Prayer and faith go hand-in-hand so where is your faith?"

I sincerely appreciate all of you who work with me to make the Word of God come to life in the lives of the readers and viewers.

God, I'm Ready to Walk in Faith

Thelma Wells

HARVEST HOUSE PUBLISHERS

EUGENE, OREGON

Unless otherwise indicated, Scripture quotations are taken from The Holy Bible, English Standard Version, copyright © 2001 by Crossway Bibles, a division of Good News Publishers. Used by permission. All rights reserved.

Verses marked NKJV are taken from the New King James Version. Copyright © 1982 by Thomas Nelson, Inc. Used by permission. All rights reserved.

Italics in Scripture quotations indicate author emphasis.

The Langston Hughes poem "Mother to Son" is from *Collected Poems*, copyright © 1994 by The Estate of Langston Hughes. Reprinted with the permission of Harold Ober Associates Incorporated.

Published in association with Van Diest Literary Agency, PO Box 1482, Sisters, Oregon 97759, www.lastchapterpublishing.com

Cover illustrations © 2010 Cartoon Resource

Cover by Koechel Peterson & Associates, Inc., Minneapolis, Minnesota

GOD, I'M READY TO WALK IN FAITH
Copyright © 2010 by Thelma Wells
Published by Harvest House Publishers
Eugene, Oregon 97402
www.harvesthousepublishers.com

Library of Congress Cataloging-in-Publication Data
Wells, Thelma.
God, I'm ready to walk in faith / Thelma Wells.
    p. cm.
ISBN 978-0-7369-3036-9 (pbk.)
1. Christian women—Religious life. I. Title.
BV4527.W4375 2011
248.8'43—dc22
                                        2010030750

Printed in the United States of America

10 11 12 13 14 15 16 17 18 19 20 / BP-SK / 10 9 8 7 6 5 4 3 2 1

Contents

What Is Faith? 7

PART 1: Faith That Trusts God with Your Family

1. Wearing Baby Shoes 11
2. Exploring One Mother's Story 19
3. Exercising Faith to Trust God More 29

PART 2: Faith That Overcomes Your Fear

4. Facing Your Fears 43
5. The Right Training 55
6. Exercising Faith to Conquer Your Fears 65

PART 3: Faith That Yields to God's Plans and Purposes

7. Wearing Grown-up Shoes 79
8. Hearing and Trusting 87
9. Exercising Faith to Accept God's Higher
   Plans and Purposes 95

PART 4: Faith That Succeeds

10. Wearing Bling-bling Shoes 113
11. Beautiful in Every Way 127
12. Exercising Faith for Your Success 141

PART 5: Faith That Fights

13. Wearing Combat Boots 151
14. For Spiritual Warfare 163
15. Exercising Faith for Spiritual Victory 173

PART 6: Faith That Sings

16. Legacy 185
17. Our Own Hall of Faith 189
18. Exercising Faith for Joyful Praise 211

What Is Faith?

Over a decade ago I was sitting in a room discussing with some friends the question of faith. One of them said she was sick of hearing about faith because it was so ambiguous. Another said she didn't even like the word "faith" because nobody can ever really define it. And the conversation continued to the tune of "I don't understand the word 'faith.'"

That conversation haunted me off and on for many years because I was stunned that people felt that way. I was even more perplexed when I learned that "faith" is found 58 times in the King James Version's Old Testament and 280 in the New Testament. Faith must be pretty important!

I was also confused by Hebrews 11:6, which states that "without faith it is impossible to please [God]" (NKJV). And the definition of faith in Hebrews 11:1 didn't make a lot of sense to me either: "Now faith is the substance of things hoped for, the evidence of things not seen" (NKJV). To help my understanding, I memorized Romans 1:16-17: "I am not ashamed of the gospel of Christ, for it is the power of God to salvation for everyone who believes, for the Jew first and also for the Greek. For in it the righteousness of God is revealed from *faith to faith*; as it is written, '*The just shall live by faith*'" (NKJV).

With this lack of understanding and all these question marks about faith, don't you think it's about time we learn everything we can about faith so we can apply it more confidently to our lives? Through Christ we've come this far by faith. Let's continue! Paul says in Romans 12:3, "For I say, through the grace given to me, to everyone who is among you, not to think of himself more highly than he ought to think, but to think soberly, as *God has dealt to each one a measure of faith*" (NKJV). In this book we will explore what faith is so we can more deeply understand how we can lean on the loving arms of the Faith-giver, knowing that he is able and willing to sustain us in every situation.

As you read, please pay close attention to the areas of your life that may cause you to question your faith. Linger there until you are assured that through faith in Jesus Christ you have freedom of mind and spirit in the situation. God is the Faith-giver, but he is also the Faith-keeper and the Faith-sustainer. He is the Faithful One!

Thelma "Mama T" Wells

PART 1

Faith That Trusts God with Your Family

1

Wearing Baby Shoes

I love shoes. I've got a closet full of them. In fact, I buy clothes just to go with my shoes! Right now I've got shoes in mind because I'm thinking about our journey through life and the shoes we wear as we walk along the pathway. I'm wondering what those shoes would say if shoes could talk. What stories would they tell?

Would your shoes speak of how you've walked through the valley of the shadow of death? Would they relate how you've trudged through graveyards of confusion? Would they tell of your travels in regions of sadness, and hurt, and grief, and trauma?

What would your shoes say?

And where will our shoes be taking you and me as we step forward into the future? What joys, what hardships, what struggles, what challenges, and what adventures are we about to walk into?

Your Desire—and Mine Too

Whatever's to come, I want to tell you that because of everything God has taught me in my many years, there's something I can say with more certainty than ever:

God, I'm ready to walk in faith!

I've been through many trials and tribulations, but here I am today ready to walk, willing to walk, and hoping to walk forever in faith. I know that's your desire as well because you've opened this book. So I want to thank you for sharing this time with me as we strengthen our faith from the Word of God.

Because I'm a visual person, I have to write things down—and so I invite you to do the same. In the pages to come, whenever you encounter questions that we'll be considering together, please take a moment to reflect on your thoughts and situation and write down your best answer in the space that's provided. I know you'll be glad you did because that's the best way to truly retain what you're learning.

Baby Shoes

Baby shoes have got to be some of the cutest things we ever see, aren't they? You may not remember when black patent leather high-tops were considered the very finest in baby shoes, but I do. I wore shoes like that! Let me tell you more about that time in my life, including some things that took me quite a while to discover.

When I was in my thirties, I went on a mission trip—my first venture outside the United States. To obtain a passport, I needed a birth certificate, and I didn't have one. So I went down to the Bureau of Vital Statistics to try to get a copy of it. When I gave them the name I grew up with, they could find no record that matched it.

It took some digging around before we finally discovered that my *real* last name—the one I received legally at birth—was not the same as the name I grew up with. The confusion arose out of the circumstances surrounding my birth. It took place in 1941, and my mother was an unwed teenager. (I'll tell you more about that later.) Eventually I had to take legal steps to clear up the records and become lawfully on paper the person I thought I always was.

Oh, but let me tell you something I'm assured of: *God* always knew who I was! And he never gave me the labels that people often give to a child born out of wedlock. I love God's truth about me—and about all of us—that's found in Psalm 139:13-17. These words from David are indeed an encouragement for me and I hope for you:

You formed my inward parts;
you knitted me together in my mother's womb.
I praise you, for I am fearfully and wonderfully made.
Wonderful are your works; my soul knows it very well.
My frame was not hidden from you,
when I was being made in secret,
intricately woven in the depths of the earth.
Your eyes saw my unformed substance;
in your book were written, every one of them,
the days that were formed for me,
when as yet there was none of them.
How precious to me are your thoughts, O God!
How vast is the sum of them!

You see, God has always known when we were going to be born, and to whom we were going to be born, and how things were going to work out—down to the last detail. He knew that my mother, a crippled teenager, was going to be unable to properly care for me. She was paralyzed on one side and had a deformed right arm and leg. When she had me, her parents put her out of the house. For a while I lived with her in the servant quarters of a large house where she worked as a maid.

When I was two, both she and I became ill. My mother called her mother and asked if she would take me and nurse me back to health. And although my grandmother refused, my grandfather called his mother—my great-grandmother—and asked her to take me and care for me in my sickness. She agreed even though she was already more than 60 years old.

I like to say now that I never did recover from that sickness—because I never went back to my mother! I lived all the rest of my childhood with my great-grandmother. I called her Granny, and it was such a wonderful experience. She was a saintly woman of God. She loved God, and she took me to church seven days a week. That's how I learned very early in life the hymns of the church.

Sometimes I would go visit my grandmother—the woman who had refused to nurse me back to health when I was two. When my grandfather would go to work, my grandmother would put me in a dark, dingy closet all day. Thankfully, because of how my saintly great-grandmother was raising me, I was able to sing the hymns of the church in that closet so I wouldn't be afraid. And when I got out of that closet, I had no trauma, no anger, no bitterness—none of that. Why? Because it was a God setup. *God met me in that closet.* He protected my mind, he protected my heart, he protected me from the things that could have happened had I not been raised by a godly great-grandmother.

Are you aware that when we go through stuff in life—the things that hurt us and discourage us—that it's really a God setup?

I'm so thankful to God right now that I was entrusted to the care of my great-grandmother. She loved me so much that for the rest of my life I thought of her as my mother.

What Are Your Thoughts?

❦ Think about the "God setups" in your life. Which of these had the most impact for you? Take a moment to write a few sentences about what these "God setups" have meant to you.

A Mother Gives Up Her Son

Do you remember Hannah's story in the Bible? As the book of 1 Samuel begins, we read about her and that she was barren. To make matters worse, her husband had another wife who was having babies and ridiculing Hannah for being childless. Hannah was distressed and distraught. In those days, if you didn't have children, you were looked down upon.

So Hannah went to the temple and prayed. She prayed desperately—so much so that the priest Eli thought she was inebriated—and he told her so. But she answered him, "No, my lord, I am a woman troubled in spirit. I have drunk neither wine nor strong drink, but I have been pouring out my soul before the LORD" (verse 15).

In her prayer that day Hannah made a vow. She promised that if God gave her a son, she would offer him back to him for all the days of his life. She wanted this child so badly, but even more than that she wanted her child to glorify God.

God, in his amazing grace and love, responded. Hannah conceived and gave birth to a baby boy. She named him Samuel. And once he was weaned, she fulfilled her vow and took him to the temple and entrusted him into Eli's care.

Now, Hannah may well have known that Eli was lacking in important parenting skills. Eli failed to bring up his own sons in the discipline and instruction of the Lord. In 1 Samuel 2:12 we read, "Now the sons of Eli were worthless men. They did not know the Lord." But that was not Hannah's concern. She was being faithful and obedient to complete her vow to God. (Anytime you make a vow to God, make sure you keep it. Ecclesiastes 5:4-5 says, "When you vow a vow to God, do not delay paying it, for he has no pleasure in fools. Pay what you vow.")

Samuel lived in the temple all his childhood, and he became such a blessing to the people of Israel. I encourage you to read his full story in the Scriptures. You will learn so much!

When I thought of how Hannah gave up her baby son, I compared it to my story. Samuel's mother and my mother gave up their babies and let someone else care for them. My mother couldn't care for her baby, but Hannah was fully able to care for hers. Yet she let her little boy go to live in the temple. Sometimes we have to make hard decisions to do what's best for our children in God's sight.

What Are Your Thoughts?

❀ What kind of hard decisions have you had to make for the sake of your family?

For a Better Life

After I'd been taken to live with my great-grandmother and was a little older, my mother sometimes had me over to spend the night. On one of these occasions I discovered that she was living in a camping tent with a dirt floor, right in the inner city of Dallas, Texas. I'd never seen anything like that before. My great-grandmother's place was a back-alley apartment, but at least it was clean and solid, and we had carpeting on the floor.

In my mother's tent were two army cots, one for my baby sister (she'd had another baby by then) and one for my mother. They had no running water, no electricity, and no phone. I was a little afraid to be there. I wasn't sure how to adapt and adjust to this, but that night I slept with my sister on her cot.

My mother was a determined woman who didn't like asking anybody for anything. She was dedicated to providing for herself any way she had to. And her independence was such that her parents didn't know she was living in that tent. But the next morning when we all woke up, she said to me, "Thelma, you don't belong here. There's a better life for you." She went next door to use the phone and called her father—my granddaddy—to come and pick me up and take me home. I was fine with that. (I learned later that out of the love of her daddy, on that very day my mother was packed up and moved out of that tent.)

I'm thankful that my mother loved me enough to send me back to the environment I'd grown to love. My great-grandmother always said to me, "Baby, your momma never gave you away; she just let me keep you for a while." Isn't that sweet?

I can imagine Hannah talking to her son and telling him, "Baby Samuel, I love you with an everlasting love. But there's something better for you; there's something better in the temple. God wants to use you in his service. I'm not walking away from you. I'm not throwing you away. I'm giving you to the best person I can—and that's Jehovah God."

If you've had to make a tough decision about your children's care, remember: *God understands*. He sees. He loves. He holds you and directs you. He says to you, "You're mine, and I love you. I'll never leave you or forsake you."

What Are Your Thoughts?

✿ Look at the following scriptures that have been stored up for our remembrance and our blessing. Reflect and write on these words God speaks to the hearts of his people.

❀ You are precious in my eyes, and honored, and I love you (Isaiah 43:4).

❀ "With everlasting love I will have compassion on you," says the LORD, your Redeemer (Isaiah 54:8).

❀ I have loved you with an everlasting love; therefore I have continued my faithfulness to you (Jeremiah 31:3).

✿ Altogether, what do these passages speak to your heart about God's attitude toward you?

✿ Yes, God really does love you. And he has proven that love in the most profound way. Meditate on this following passage:

You were ransomed...not with perishable things such as silver or gold, but with the precious blood of Christ, like that of a lamb without blemish or spot...Through him [you] are believers in God, who raised him from the

dead and gave him glory, so that your faith and hope are
in God (1 Peter 1:18-19,21).

❀ On the basis of these wonderful words, what exactly has God
done for the sake of establishing your faith and your hope in
him? Explain this in your own way.

2

Exploring One Mother's Story

If you've read the book of Judges and seen the background of the times
leading up to the events in 1 Samuel (Hannah's story), then you know
that Israel had endured a long history of instability and confusion.
Israel needed strong and upright leadership to move forward into a
new era—and Samuel, Hannah's son, would be God's man to provide
that leadership.

I encourage you to open your heart and learn from the account of
Hannah. Her story is one of the best portraits of godly, faithful moth-
erhood in all of Scripture!

As mentioned previously, Hannah was barren, and she suffered
anguish and humiliation for it. She took her situation to the Lord:

> She was deeply distressed and prayed to the LORD and
> wept bitterly. And she vowed a vow and said, "O LORD
> of hosts, if you will indeed look on the affliction of your
> servant and remember me and not forget your servant,
> but will give to your servant a son, then I will give him
> to the LORD all the days of his life" (1 Samuel 1:10-11).

The next verse tells us that Hannah "*continued* praying before the
LORD." And later, when she explained her manner of praying to Eli the

priest (who thought she was drunk), she told him, "Do not regard your servant as a worthless woman, for all along I have been speaking out of my great anxiety and vexation" (verse 16).

What Are Your Thoughts?

❦ Although Hannah was so upset, how did those verses from 1 Samuel demonstrate her true faith in God?

❦ What did Hannah believe about God that caused her to pray the way she did?

❀ The following passages from the book of Psalms were written after Hannah's time, but they reflect her beliefs about her heavenly Father:

> Who is like the LORD our God…He gives the barren woman a home, making her the joyous mother of children. Praise the Lord! (Psalm 113:5,9).

> Behold, children are a heritage from the LORD, the fruit of the womb a reward (Psalm 127:3).

❀ Now read what happened after Hannah spoke to Eli to clarify his mistaken perception of her:

> Then Eli answered, "Go in peace, and the God of Israel grant your petition that you have made to him."

> And she said, "Let your servant find favor in your eyes." Then the woman went her way and ate, and her face was no longer sad.

They rose early in the morning and worshiped before the LORD; then they went back to their house at Ramah. And Elkanah knew Hannah his wife, and the LORD remembered her. And in due time Hannah conceived and bore a son, and she called his name Samuel, for she said, "I have asked for him from the LORD" (1 Samuel 1:17-20).

🌼 What clues and evidence regarding Hannah's faith did you see in that passage?

🌼 Now read about the time Hannah brought her son to Eli and the temple to fulfill her vow and give him back to the Lord:

The man Elkanah and all his house went up to offer to the LORD the yearly sacrifice and to pay his vow. But Hannah did not go up, for she said to her husband, "As soon as the child is weaned, I will bring him, so that he may appear in the presence of the LORD and dwell there forever."

Elkanah her husband said to her, "Do what seems best to you; wait until you have weaned him; only, may the LORD establish his word."

So the woman remained and nursed her son until she weaned him. And when she had weaned him, she took him up with her...to the house of the LORD at Shiloh. And the child was young. Then they slaughtered the bull, and they brought the child to Eli.

And she said, "Oh, my lord! As you live, my lord, I am the woman who was standing here in your presence, praying to the LORD. For this child I prayed,

and the LORD has granted me my petition that I
made to him. Therefore I have lent him to the LORD.
As long as he lives, he is lent to the LORD" (1 Samuel 1:21-28).

❀ Once more, what evidence of Hannah's faith did you find in
that passage?

❊ What stands out to you the most regarding Hannah's faith?

❊ What aspects of Hannah's faith would you like to have in your life?
Express your desire in a written prayer to your heavenly Father.

Reason to Sing

When we continue on with Hannah's story in 1 Samuel 2, we find
her praising God in a prayer that's like a mighty hymn of praise. Her
song begins with these wonderful lines:

My heart exults in the LORD;
my strength is exalted in the LORD...
There is none holy like the LORD;
there is none besides you;
there is no rock like our God (1 Samuel 2:1-2).

Can you see what a high and wonderful view she had of God? What
a woman of faith! She went on in her song to direct a few words toward
those who are proud and arrogant in their opposition to the Lord. And

she continued boasting of the Lord—what he does and what he will do in the future:

> Talk no more so very proudly,
>   let not arrogance come from your mouth;
> for the LORD is a God of knowledge,
>   and by him actions are weighed.
> The bows of the mighty are broken,
>   but the feeble bind on strength.
> Those who were full have hired themselves out for bread,
>   but those who were hungry have ceased to hunger.
> The barren has borne seven,
>   but she who has many children is forlorn.
> The LORD kills and brings to life;
>   he brings down to Sheol and raises up.
> The LORD makes poor and makes rich;
>   he brings low and he exalts.
> He raises up the poor from the dust;
>   he lifts the needy from the ash heap
> to make them sit with princes
>   and inherit a seat of honor.
> For the pillars of the earth are the LORD's,
>   and on them he has set the world.
> He will guard the feet of his faithful ones,
>   but the wicked shall be cut off in darkness,
>   for not by might shall a man prevail.
> The adversaries of the LORD shall be broken to pieces;
>   against them he will thunder in heaven.
> The LORD will judge the ends of the earth;
>   he will give strength to his king
>   and exalt the power of his anointed
>   (1 Samuel 2:3-10).

In these rich words of praise that flow from Hannah's lips, can you see how insightful her faith is? And what a comprehensive view she has of God?

What Are Your Thoughts?

❀ From the picture of Hannah's faith that is revealed in her words of praise, write down the truths about God that most impress *you*— truths that Hannah understood so profoundly.

When our faith is growing toward the richness and depth of Hannah's faith, we just can't help singing the Lord's praises! In my childhood, when I had to stay in that closet in my grandmother's house, I would sing the hymns and songs I'd learned in church and from my great-grandmother. I learned about God's love and godly principles by singing those songs, and that's why (I know now) I have no trauma from being locked in that closet.

Since then, I've learned to sing in all the closets of life. I've had a lot of stuff happen; I've walked a lot of troublesome trails. But through the trials of life I've discovered that God will dispatch his ministering angels to keep watch over me and protect me.

The hardships that have come my way are substantial enough for me to tell you with certainty that when life gets tough, you have to decide where you're going to walk. Are you going to walk in faith? Are you going to step forward trusting in God? Are you going to lean on his everlasting arms? Will your faith be real enough that you can keep on singing praises to him?

I love to sing! In fact, I still sing "Jesus loves me!" every day.

God's Best Work

We looked earlier at Psalm 139, where David says to the Lord, "I praise you, for I am fearfully and wonderfully made" (verse 14). As a little girl I didn't know that scripture, but I *felt* that I was fearfully and wonderfully made. I knew I was because my great-grandmother loved me enough to teach me not only the hymns of the church but also the Word of God. And throughout the Word of God there is an underlying assumption and insistence that all of us, being created by God, are indeed special. Each one of us is an awesome wonder. Just look at this verse: "For we are his workmanship, created in Christ Jesus for good works, which God prepared beforehand, that we should walk in them" (Ephesians 2:10). We are God's best work!

What Are Your Thoughts?

- If you do trust God for this truth, write a statement of faith about who you are and who God created you to be. Start with "I believe I am…" and finish with your personal translation of Ephesians 2:10.

  I believe I am…

No Crystal Stair

Knowing that we're God's best work is a vibrant part of our faith that will help keep us walking forward even when the journey gets uncomfortable. And that's going to happen. I like this poem by Langston Hughes, where a mother is speaking to her son:

> Well, son, I'll tell you:
> Life for me ain't been no crystal stair.
> It's had tacks in it,
> And splinters,
> And boards torn up,
> And places with no carpet on the floor—
> Bare.
> But all the time
> I'se been a-climbin' on,
> And reachin' landin's,
> And turnin' corners,
> And sometimes goin' in the dark
> Where there ain't been no light.

So, boy, don't you turn back.
Don't you set down on the steps.
'Cause you finds it's kinder hard.
Don't you fall now—
For I'se still goin', honey,
I'se still climbin',
And life for me ain't been no crystal stair
[used by permission].

Life is no crystal stair, but when we walk in faith we'll keep climbing, we'll keep reaching, we'll keep stepping forward. We'll walk where others fear to tread. And one of these days we'll step out fully into the glorious final destiny God has for us. So keep going, and don't turn back! God will be with you; I know he will. Your steps will be "ordered by the LORD," and he'll take great delight in your journey (Psalm 37:23 NKJV).

What Are Your Thoughts?

✺ Listen to the *promises* in these words from the Lord to his people:

> The LORD will keep your going out and your coming in from this time forth and forevermore (Psalm 121:8).

> Trust in the LORD with all your heart, and do not lean on your own understanding. In all your ways acknowledge him, and he will make straight your paths (Proverbs 3:5-6).

❀ By the authority of the Word of God, you can be certain that he wants to do these things for *you* as you walk with him in faith. Express these verses in your own words. What does the Lord want to do personally for *you*?

Daily Doorways

One of my prayers for my daily journey is, "Lord, close the doors I don't need to walk through today, and open the doors I need to walk through. And put in my path the people you want me to interact with." We need to pray this prayer or one like it because we sometimes head down paths God doesn't want us to walk in. We walk in paths that end up being hurtful, or confusing, or frustrating, or aggravating, or agitating, or humiliating, or impoverishing. But he'll come beside us and show us the way of escape from those wrong directions. And that gives us new reasons to thank and praise him!

What Are Your Thoughts?

❊ I hope you can fully appreciate the following prayers from the book of Psalms. They're such a blessing for helping us offer up our daily path into the hands of the Lord.

> Let me hear in the morning of your steadfast love,
> for in you I trust.
> Make me know the way I should go,
> for to you I lift up my soul…
> Teach me to do your will,
> for you are my God!
> Let your good Spirit lead me on level ground!
> (Psalm 143:8,10).

> Make me to know your ways, O LORD;
> teach me your paths.
> Lead me in your truth and teach me,
> for you are the God of my salvation;
> for you I wait all the day long
> (Psalm 25:4-5).

❊ Can you see why these are such good prayers for anyone who's ready to walk in faith? Which of the requests in these verses do you think will be the most valuabmle for *you* to remember and repeat?

Let's Pray

O God, how awesome and glorious you are! How we love your guidance and your protection! Thank you again for your love—a love so great that you gave your Son for us, that we might be adopted by you into your kingdom. Thank you, Father. In Jesus' name. Amen.

3

Exercising Faith to Trust God More

Faith takes careful effort. Faith takes exercise. *Faith takes work.* I hope that's something you know and won't overlook. Faith isn't something we can take for granted or let happen:

> But you, beloved, *build yourselves up in your most holy faith;* pray in the Holy Spirit; keep yourselves in the love of God, waiting for the mercy of our Lord Jesus Christ that leads to eternal life (Jude 20-21).

What Are Your Thoughts?

As you reflect on that verse, think about your life. How is each of the following meant to be connected to *your* faith in a practical way?

prayer—

the Holy Spirit—

feeling loved by God—

expecting mercy from the Lord—

As we gain confidence in affirming "Lord, I'm ready to walk by faith!" I will help you interact with the Word of God so you can discover more about *exercising* your faith. We'll do that together in this chapter before we move to Part 2 of this book.

Someone to Trust

Faith means *trusting*.

And trusting requires knowing.

You really can't trust someone you don't know. Have you thought about that? This is a good reminder that getting to know God better is the best way to learn to trust him more, and that will build up our faith.

What Are Your Thoughts?

❀ Each of the following passages is a personal message to you from your Lord and your God, letting you know what he is like and what he wants to *do for you* and *be for you*. Take a moment and respond to each of these messages with your own words of reflection, appreciation, gratitude, and understanding.

It is the LORD who goes before *you*. He will be with *you*; he will not leave *you* or forsake *you*. Do not fear or be dismayed (Deuteronomy 31:8)—

When *you* pass through the waters, I will be with *you*; and through the rivers, they shall not overwhelm *you*; when *you* walk through fire *you* shall not be burned, and the flame shall not consume *you* (Isaiah 43:2)—

"For the mountains may depart and the hills be removed, but my steadfast love shall not depart from *you*, and my covenant of peace shall not be removed," says the LORD (Isaiah 54:10)—

[Jesus said,] "If *you* ask me anything in my name, I will do it" (John 14:14)—

My grace is sufficient for *you*, for my power is made perfect in weakness (2 Corinthians 12:9)—

For sin will have no dominion over *you*, since *you* are not under law but under grace (Romans 6:14)—

He has said, "I will never leave *you* nor forsake *you*" (Hebrews 13:5)—

- Praise the Lord! He gives us such wonderful promises in his Word to savor and study and treasure in our hearts.

Enjoying All That He Is

Everything God wants to do for you, and all that he wants to be for you, flows out of *who he is*—his character and personality. In his great love for us, he reveals so much about himself in his Word. He so wants us to know him as he really is.

What Are Your Thoughts?

- In each of the following passages, God tells us something about himself that can help us deepen our faith in him and our love for him. Accept each one of these statements as the Lord's personal message to you about who he is. Then take a moment and respond sincerely and fully to each of these passages in new and fresh ways. Write down your own words of reflection, appreciation, gratitude, and understanding.

  The Lord, the Lord, a God merciful and gracious, slow to anger, and abounding in steadfast love and faithfulness (Exodus 34:6)—

  The word of the Lord proves true; he is a shield for all those who take refuge in him (Psalm 18:30)—

For he satisfies the longing soul, and the hungry soul he fills with good things (Psalm 107:9)—

Turn to me and be saved, all the ends of the earth! For I am God, and there is no other (Isaiah 45:22)—

I am the LORD who practices steadfast love, justice, and righteousness in the earth. For in these things I delight, declares the LORD (Jeremiah 9:24)—

Oh, the depth of the riches and wisdom and knowledge of God! How unsearchable are his judgments and how inscrutable his ways! "For who has known the mind of the Lord, or who has been his counselor?" "Or who has given a gift to him that he might be repaid?" For from him and through him and to him are all things (Romans 11:33-36)—

Now to him who is able to do far more abundantly than all that we ask or think, according to the power at work within us, to him be glory in the church and in Christ Jesus throughout all generations, forever and ever. Amen (Ephesians 3:20-21)—

Every good gift and every perfect gift is from above, coming down from the Father of lights with whom there is
no variation or shadow due to change (James 1:17)—

Full Faith in All of God

Listen to these words that Jesus uttered with a loud cry: "Whoever
believes in me, believes not in me but in him who sent me. And whoever sees me sees him who sent me" (John 12:44).

What Are Your Thoughts?

✿ What does it mean to you that your faith is not in Jesus alone, but
also in his Father?

✿ Why do you think Jesus thought it so important to make this point
so clear?

✿ What does it mean to you that God the Father is the ultimate "tar-
get" and object of *all* your faith?

Faith has been described by biblical scholar Alexander Souter as "the
leaning of your entire human personality on Him in absolute trust and
confidence in His power, wisdom, and goodness."

What Are Your Thoughts?

❊ How do you go about "leaning your personality" on God? What does this involve?

Choosing to Trust

What Are Your Thoughts?

❊ Study the following words from songs that Israel's King David wrote. How does each verse show David's conscious decision to trust in the Lord? What was going on in his mind and in his will?

> I have set the LORD always before me; because he is at my right hand, I shall not be shaken (Psalm 16:8)—

> O my God, in you I trust; let me not be put to shame; let not my enemies exult over me (Psalm 25:2)—

> In God I trust; I shall not be afraid. What can man do to me? (Psalm 56:11)—

❊ Some important dynamics of personal trust in the Lord are laid out for us in these words written by the prophet Isaiah:

You keep him in perfect peace whose mind is stayed on you, because he trusts in you. Trust in the LORD forever, for the LORD God is an everlasting rock (Isaiah 26:3-4).

❀ What are the most important lessons to learn about trusting personally in the Lord?

Facts About Trusting

Is trusting God really worth it? Maybe sometimes you wonder; but of course you know it *is* worth it in the long run, even if sometimes we don't *feel* like it is right now.

What Are Your Thoughts?

✿ The following verses give us some *facts* about trusting God. In each passage, identify the fact and then express it in your own words.

Those who know your name put their trust in you, for you, O LORD, have not forsaken those who seek you (Psalm 9:10)—

Their idols [of the nations] are silver and gold, the work of human hands. They have mouths, but do not speak; eyes, but do not see. They have ears, but do not hear; noses, but do not smell. They have hands, but do not feel; feet, but do not walk; and they do not make a sound in their throat. Those who make them become like them; so do all who trust in them (Psalm 115:4-8)—

It is better to take refuge in the LORD than to trust in man. It is better to take refuge in the LORD than to trust in princes (Psalm 118:8-9)—

Those who trust in the LORD are like Mount Zion, which cannot be moved, but abides forever (Psalm 125:1)—

And the effect of righteousness will be peace, and the result of righteousness, quietness and trust forever (Isaiah 32:17)—

Blessed is the man who trusts in the LORD, whose trust is the LORD (Jeremiah 17:7)—

Affirmations of Trust

What Are Your Thoughts?

❀ The following passages contain affirmations to encourage and strengthen your soul. Use them to talk and write directly to the One who is your everlasting trust.

In the LORD I take refuge (Psalm 11:1)—

I shall behold your face in righteousness; when I awake, I
shall be satisfied with your likeness (Psalm 17:15)—

When I am afraid, I put my trust in you. In God, whose
word I praise, in God I trust; I shall not be afraid. What
can flesh do to me? (Psalm 56:3-4)—

I will say to the LORD, "My refuge and my fortress, my
God, in whom I trust" (Psalm 91:2)—

Let your steadfast love come to me, O LORD, your salvation according to your promise; then shall I have an
answer for him who taunts me, for I trust in your word
(Psalm 119:41-42)—

Let me hear in the morning of your steadfast love, for in
you I trust. Make me know the way I should go, for to
you I lift up my soul (Psalm 143:8)—

Commands and Invitations to Trust

I hope you remember that every command from the Lord is an invitation to a higher experience. He never commands us to do anything

that he doesn't also equip us to carry out. So with a full and open heart, receive what the Lord invites you to do in the following passages.

What Are Your Thoughts?

✖ Write your responses to God's personal invitations to you.

Trust in the LORD, and do good; dwell in the land and befriend faithfulness (Psalm 37:3)—

Commit your way to the LORD; trust in him, and he will act (Psalm 37:5)—

Cast your burden on the LORD, and he will sustain you; he will never permit the righteous to be moved (Psalm 55:22)—

Trust in him at all times, O people; pour out your heart before him; God is a refuge for us (Psalm 62:8)—

Put not your trust in princes, in a son of man, in whom there is no salvation. When his breath departs, he returns to the earth; on that very day his plans perish (Psalm 146:3-4)—

> Trust in the LORD with all your heart, and do not lean on
> your own understanding (Proverbs 3:5)—

It's good to remember also that we're actually commanded—*invited*—to practice faith (as well as love), as the apostle John tells us:

> And *this is his commandment*, that we *believe* in the name
> of his Son Jesus Christ and love one another, just as he
> has commanded us (1 John 3:23).

And it's by the living presence of the Lord within us that we are able to keep his commands:

> Whoever keeps his commandments abides in him, and
> he in them. And by this we know that he abides in us, by
> the Spirit whom he has given us (1 John 3:24).

His presence is sure and certain. By faith—and by the Spirit—*we know.*

PART 2

Faith That Overcomes Your Fear

4

Facing Your Fears

I knew who my daddy was while I was growing up, but I didn't know a lot about what he did. One thing I did know: Every Christmas he would bring us a ham. So at least he showed up once a year. But all during my growing up years I was blessed to have positive male figures in my life, especially my great-grandfather and grandfather. Those two men were powerful influences in my life. And both of them, with affection, called me "Pooch."

Treasures of Trust

I loved being with my great-grandfather because I had the privilege of walking with him, hand-in-hand, taking him to church or to Tapplets' Fish Market or to Garner's Ice Cream Parlor. He would say, "Pooch, you want some ice cream today?" Then off we'd go. The neighbors would say, "There goes that blind man with that little girl."

He was so sweet to me. We used to play prayer meeting together. At church, when my great-grandfather started praying, nobody wanted to be caught standing and waiting to be seated 'cause he would pray and pray and pray and pray…and then pray some more.

So when he and I enjoyed the blessing of playing prayer meeting together, I had a partner with impressive experience. As we played, I would sing some church songs I was learning and make up the words I didn't know.

My great-grandfather taught me the Twenty-third Psalm and the Lord's Prayer (I've taught them to my children as well—and I hope they're teaching theirs). Yes, those wonderful treasures of truth, those nuggets of gold, those diamonds—I had the privilege of learning from my great-granddaddy.

Here's something else he did for me. There were times when I was afraid to go to my room or to be alone because I thought I'd been seeing or hearing the boogie man. So one day when I was dealing with that fear, my great-granddaddy called to me from the screened-in front porch of our upstairs apartment.

"Pooch, baby, come here."

I went to him, and he asked, "Do you want to get rid of that boogie man?"

I said, "Yes sir." I believed he could help me do that because he had earned my trust.

"This is what I want you to do," he told me. "I want you to close your eyes, and I want you to repeat the Twenty-third Psalm and the Lord's Prayer, one right after the other, over and over until you don't feel any fear." And he added, "Now, Pooch, you're going to get rid of that fear *today*."

So I followed his instructions. There on that screened-in porch, I closed my eyes and started repeating the Twenty-third Psalm: "The Lord is my shepherd, I shall not want…" When I finished it, I launched into the Lord's Prayer: "Our Father, who art in heaven, hallowed be thy name…" I repeated them one after the other, over and over, just as he said—and I quickly found myself experiencing release and relief.

When I opened up my eyes and looked upward through the screen into the sky, I saw the clouds billowing white, so soft and sweet on a sunshiny day. And those clouds had formed the outline of the head of Jesus! I can still see that image in my mind's eye. Whenever I get a notion to possibly become afraid, I remember what I saw that afternoon.

Now I have to admit that I haven't entirely conquered every fear. Mice really do bother me. I'm genuinely afraid of them, and I'm asking God to release me from that fear. Meanwhile, I never invite mice into my house—not at all.

But I thank God for all the fear that he's taken away.

Do you want to know why I'm sure he's removed my fear? I've traveled all over the world by myself without fear. Once I was seated on a bench at a railway station in England, and a young man with spiked green hair and dressed in leather came over. He looked like one tough cookie. Folks around me got up and moved elsewhere, but I was tired. I thought, *If he's going to kill me, he'll just have to do it right here.*

After he sat down next to me, I said, "Hi, what's going on?"

He didn't respond, and I figured he might not recognize American phrases. So I tried again: "Hello! How are you doing?"

He started talking with me, and I discovered he was a college student working on a degree. He was very intelligent, very likable, and Welsh. I discovered I don't have to be afraid of people because of the way they look. Later we got on the same train traveling to Cardiff, Wales, and it was such a blessing to make a new friend.

No Fear

Fear is not a part of our makeup when we know God. He reminds us of that in these words:

> God gave us a spirit not of fear but of power and love and self-control (2 Timothy 1:7).

It was this spirit of power and love emanating from my great-grandfather that caused me to go and do and be more than I could have had he not shared God's grace with me.

What Are Your Thoughts?

✿ Are there fears you need deliverance from? If so, what are they?

✿ Reflect in a fresh way on these bold words of faith in Psalm 23:

The LORD is my shepherd; I shall not want.
He makes me lie down in green pastures.
He leads me beside still waters.
He restores my soul.
He leads me in paths of righteousness for his
 name's sake.
Even though I walk through the valley of the
 shadow of death,
I will fear no evil, for you are with me;
your rod and your staff, they comfort me.
You prepare a table before me in the presence of
 my enemies;
you anoint my head with oil; my cup overflows.
Surely goodness and mercy shall follow me all the
 days of my life,
and I shall dwell in the house of the LORD forever.

❈ In Psalm 23, a song from the heart of David, what are the specific truths and perspectives that are greater than all your fears and that will help you overcome your fears?

❈ Meditate on how Jesus taught his disciples to pray:

Our Father in heaven,
hallowed be your name.
Your kingdom come,
your will be done,
on earth as it is in heaven.
Give us this day our daily bread,
and forgive us our debts,
as we also have forgiven our debtors.
And lead us not into temptation,
but deliver us from evil.

❀ What are the specific truths and perspectives in this timeless prayer that are greater than all your fears and that can help you overcome your fears?

Faith Defeats Fear

God not only tells us to not be afraid, but he tells us *why* we can be free from fear. When we're trying to overcome fear, we don't just "suck it up" and try to be brave. No, we've got very good *reasons* to not be afraid! Look at these words from the Lord to his people, all from the book of Isaiah:

> Fear not, for I am with you; be not dismayed, for I am your God; I will strengthen you, I will help you, I will uphold you with my righteous right hand (41:10).

> For I, the LORD your God, hold your right hand; it is I who say to you, "Fear not, I am the one who helps you." Fear not...I am the one who helps you, declares the LORD; your Redeemer is the Holy One of Israel (41:13-14).

> Thus says the LORD, he who created you, O Jacob, he who formed you, O Israel: "Fear not, for I have redeemed you; I have called you by name, you are mine" (43:1).

> Fear not, for I am with you (43:5).

What Are Your Thoughts?

❀ In those verses from Isaiah, what were the specific reasons why God's people can be free from fear?

✷ Which of those reasons mean the most to your heart and soul?

Fear is a healthy, legitimate, God-given emotion that helps keep us safe when it's acting within its purposeful boundaries. But when it interferes with our lives or alters how we approach life, it's gone beyond what it was meant to do. Even the great patriarch Abraham dealt with fear. In Genesis 15, we enter into the middle of the story of Abraham's life. He's already received great promises from God. But now we find him fearful of the future because he's childless. He's lived a lot of years, and he's not getting any younger. Look at what God tells him one night:

> The word of the LORD came to Abram in a vision: "Fear not, Abram, I am your shield; your reward shall be very great" (Genesis 15:1).

What Are Your Thoughts?

✷ How would you feel if God said that to you when you are afraid or agitated?

✷ How applicable are these words to your situation? How is God *your* shield?

✷ How accurate is it to say you've got a great reward coming? What do you think it is?

Even after this good, strong word from the Lord that night, Abraham was still uneasy. He answered, "O Lord GOD, what will you give me, for I continue childless?...Behold, you have given me no offspring" (Genesis 15:2-3). And God responded by promising him a son of his very own. And then he asked Abraham to step outside the tent.

> And he brought him outside and said, "Look toward heaven, and number the stars, if you are able to number them." Then he said to him, "So shall your offspring be" (Genesis 15:5).

And how did Abraham respond? "He believed the LORD, and he counted it to him as righteousness" (Genesis 15:6). In that moment Abraham went from fear to faith. He was showing the way for all of us!

What Are Your Thoughts?

❈ From what you see in this example of Abraham, how do we find release from fear? What did God do to get him there? And what did Abraham do?

❈ How can you follow in Abraham's steps? What has God done for you? What does he want you to do so you can leave your fears behind and move forward in confidence?

❈ Look at what David sings about in Psalm 27:1:

> The LORD is my light and my salvation;
> whom shall I fear?
> The LORD is the stronghold of my life;
> of whom shall I be afraid?

❧ Can you sing those words confidently with David? I hope so! And when you do, what do these phrases mean to your heart and soul?

the Lord God is your *light?*

the Lord is your *salvation?*

the Lord is the *stronghold* of your life?

You can sing this too, just as I always do:

What have I to dread, what have I to fear,
Leaning on the everlasting arms;
I have blessed peace with my Lord so near,
Leaning on the everlasting arms.

Staying Positive

I mentioned earlier that both my great-grandfather and my grandfather were huge blessings in my life. Granddaddy Lawrence and I had a date almost every Saturday. He would take me to the movies. And later, when I started dating, he was my chaperone. (Amen and hallelujah for chaperones!)

I remember going with my granddaddy to the Majestic Theater in downtown Dallas. Because we weren't white, we had to go upstairs through a back door, and we sat in what they called the Buzzards' Roost. We ate the stale candy and stale popcorn and drank the unfizzed Cokes. However, I didn't know the difference because that's how I grew up.

I was kind of mischievous. We sat right under the projection booth, and in the light beaming down, you could see lint floating in the air. Sometimes I would reach up and try to catch it. My grandfather would say, "Pooch, what are you doing?" I'd shake my head and say, "Nothing." Often he would nod off and sleep through most of the movie.

Once when we were there, Granddaddy Lawrence said something to me I'll always remember. "Pooch, one of these days you're not going to have to go through the back door. You're not going to have to sit in the Buzzards' Roost. And you're going to have fresh candy and freshly popped popcorn." Then he said, "You will! Just keep living, Pooch."

Occasionally he took me to the bank where he worked as a custodian. The bank had separate water fountains labeled "white" and "colored," and they had segregated bathrooms too. I wondered what was different about the white water. When I slipped over to the white fountain and tried it, I discovered that the only difference was the temperature; "white" water was cool and "colored" water wasn't.

Granddaddy Lawrence told me, "Pooch, one of these days, you're going to be able to walk to a clean water fountain anywhere and drink as much water as you want, for as long as you want. Just keep living! You'll be able to do that."

He was so positive. In fact, I grew up with a lot of positive people around. I was raised in a community where people watched out for one another and encouraged each other.

And as the years passed by, there came the day when I had the privilege of walking through the big front doors of the Majestic Theater. I went down the aisle and sat in the front row center. I didn't have to sit in the Buzzards' Roost anymore. Oh, I thank God for my great-granddaddy and granddaddy, who were kind enough to teach me to have hope and believe in a better future.

I hope you were as privileged as I was to grow up in a positive environment that fostered hope. But I'm not blind to reality. I know that this is *not* the childhood experience of so many, many people. And maybe it wasn't your experience either. Maybe the negatives far outweighed the positives in the environment that shaped your outlook on life. *But that's no obstacle to God!* Our God is the God of hope—of miraculous hope. And he's ready to root that hope and nurture it deep in your soul so it grows tall and strong.

Are you hungry for hope? Are you desperate for more positivity? This is my prayer for you:

> May the God of hope fill you with all joy and peace in believing, so that by the power of the Holy Spirit you may abound in hope (Romans 15:13).

Yes, God can *fill* you with *abounding* hope—with a hope that overflows with joy and peace. That's our Father's love-gift to every son and daughter of his who's ready to walk in faith.

What Are Your Thoughts?

❧ Do you believe that God will give you abounding hope that overflows with joy and peace? Are you able to trust him for that? Talk to him about it, and write down the words that flow from your heart.

Be willing to patiently wait for God's gift of hope to unfold for you in all its fullness. Take these words to heart:

> For you, O LORD, do I wait;
> it is you, O LORD my God,
> who will answer (Psalm 38:15).

> I wait for the LORD, my soul waits, and in his word
> I hope; my soul waits for the LORD more than watch-
> men for the morning, more than watchmen for the
> morning (Psalm 130:5-6).

Meanwhile, you can make his work easier by taking hold of true and personal affirmations from his Word.

What Are Your Thoughts?

✳ The following statements about our *true identity* are God's gifts for us. Take each verse and express it in your own words as a personal affirmation about yourself. For example, Romans 6:11 tells us, "So you also must consider yourselves dead to sin and alive to God in Christ Jesus." As a personal affirmation, I can write it this way: "In Christ Jesus I consider myself dead to sin and alive in God!"

> Since we have been justified by faith, we have peace with God through our Lord Jesus Christ (Romans 5:1).

> For the law of the Spirit of life has set you free in Christ Jesus from the law of sin and death (Romans 8:2).

> The Spirit himself bears witness with our spirit that we are children of God (Romans 8:16).

> Now we have received not the spirit of the world, but the Spirit who is from God, that we might understand the things freely given us by God (1 Corinthians 2:12).

> We all, with unveiled face, beholding the glory of the Lord, are being transformed into the same image from one degree of glory to another. For this comes from the Lord who is the Spirit (2 Corinthians 3:18).

- For we are his workmanship, created in Christ Jesus for good works, which God prepared beforehand, that we should walk in them (Ephesians 2:10).

For at one time you were darkness, but now you are light in the Lord (Ephesians 5:8).

See what kind of love the Father has given to us, that we should be called children of God (1 John 3:1).

✿ Which of those affirmations are the most important for you to remind yourself of again and again and again?

5

The Right Training

There's a certain man of faith in the Bible who has always fascinated me. His life is a testimony to the truth of this scripture: "Train up a child in the way he should go; even when he is old he will not depart from it" (Proverbs 22:6).

Let me clarify something. This verse doesn't say that the child you train up correctly won't act crazy sometimes, or won't be strong-willed, or will never stray. But if you train up children in the right way, the things of God will always be in their minds. Nothing can take that knowledge away from them. They will never forget the things of the Lord that they were taught by you and others.

We don't need to worry about our children. God knows all about them, and he cares for them. Remember that he promises blessings to the children of the righteous (see Psalms 25:12-13; 37:25-26; 112:1-2; Proverbs 20:7).

The man of faith I want to tell you about is someone who, as a boy, had a lot of women around him vying for his attention. He was a Hebrew, born to a woman named Jochebed. Do you know who I'm talking about yet?

Yes, I'm talking about Moses! Moses' story includes a lot of women! As the story of Moses begins, at the start of the book of Exodus, we see two Hebrew midwives (1:15-21). Pharaoh had decreed that these midwives were to kill all the newborn boys among the Hebrews, but these women didn't do that. And when the king asked for an explanation, they made up an excuse: "Those Hebrew women have babies so fast! We just don't get there in time." And God honored these midwives for saving many babies.

The next woman we read about in Moses' life is his mother. She gave birth and then hid little Moses for three months. Can you imagine having a baby less than three months old and trying to hide him? *Waaaa! Waaaaa! Waaaahhh!* We learn later that Moses' mother's name was Jochebed. God had a plan for this child, and his mother must surely have sensed that fact. She knew this little Hebrew boy wasn't like other Hebrew boys. When Moses was three months old and she could hide him no longer, she came up with an ingenious idea. She made a thatched basket and put Moses inside. (I guess you could say he was a basket case!) Then she sat that basket in the water of the River Nile among the reeds. Moses' older sister, Miriam (another female!), stood a little ways off to watch over the babe.

Then along came another woman—an Egyptian princess, the daughter of Pharaoh, along with her attendants. This princess saw the basket and sent a servant over to see what it was. When the servant brought it to her and she opened the basket, she saw a baby boy. Although she recognized it as a Hebrew child, she thought, *Mine!* And no wonder, for all through Scripture we read how attractive this baby boy was: "the child was beautiful" (Hebrews 11:23); "he was a fine child" (Exodus 2:2); "he was beautiful in God's sight" (Acts 7:20).

The princess wasn't able to nurse this fine-looking baby, but right then Miriam stepped forward with a plan. She said she knew somebody who could nurse this baby. So the princess let this girl take the baby to be cared for in his infancy. Miriam, of course, took her little brother back to their mother. Moses got the chance to be nursed and encouraged and nurtured at home by his own mother—and Jochebed got paid for it with money from Pharaoh's household!

As this little boy grew, I can just imagine Jochebed teaching him Hebrew customs and traditions and the promises of the Lord. Eventually, when he was weaned, he was taken into the palace and grew up as the child of Pharaoh's daughter. There he got the best education possible: "Moses was instructed in all the wisdom of the Egyptians" (Acts 7:22). But you know, he'd already gotten an education, thanks to his godly mother.

And it's easy to conjecture that what he learned from his true mother, Jochebed, about the Hebrew faith and culture caused him to defend a Hebrew and later decide to serve the Lord. Look at what he did:

> By faith Moses, when he was grown up, refused to be called the son of Pharaoh's daughter, choosing rather to be mistreated with the people of God than to enjoy the fleeting pleasures of sin. He considered the reproach of Christ greater wealth than the treasures of Egypt, for he was looking to the reward (Hebrews 11:24-26).

Think for a minute about that. Isn't it wonderful that Moses was able to live for the future instead of the present? By the grace of God he was able to look forward to Jesus Christ, and he was able to look forward to his own reward.

What Are Your Thoughts?

✿ What do *you* look forward to? What do you want to keep in your mind and heart as a vision for the future so that you're not just living for the present moment?

Time to Go Back

Moses had been brought up "in the way he should go." He had a heart for what he knew was right in the sight of God. When he was a young adult, Moses killed an Egyptian who'd been beating a Hebrew (Exodus 2:11-15). He had to flee Egypt because he would be executed for murdering an Egyptian. So he went to a place called Midian, and there he found seven pretty girls. *Hmmm!* These pretty girls were at a well to get water for their father's flock. But they were being prevented from doing so by some rowdy shepherds. And here comes Moses on the scene, and yes, he stands up for those young women. He not only protects them, he helps them draw water from the well and fill the livestock's water troughs. When Jethro's daughter told him about Moses, he told them to bring him home to join them for supper. Jethro (also called Reuel in Exodus) accepted Moses into his home and gave him the eldest of his daughters, Zipporah, to be his wife.

Moses was 40 years old when he fled Egypt. And 40 years after that, God did something really strange. He started a fire in a bush, and he called, "Moses, Moses!" He commanded Moses to come close and take off his shoes because that ground where he was standing was holy. God told Moses he wanted him to go back to Egypt and tell Pharaoh, "Let my people go!" (You can read all about this in Exodus 3 and 4.)

But Moses had a problem with that. He said he wasn't good at talking. Can't you just imagine God rolling his eyes and saying, "Duh! I know that." He told Moses he'd already created somebody to do the talking for him—his older brother Aaron.

While we're thinking about Moses, we've got to take a moment to review that wonderful passage where God spoke about his name to Moses:

> Then Moses said to God, "If I come to the people of Israel and say to them, 'The God of your fathers has sent me to you,' and they ask me, 'What is his name?' what shall I say to them?"

> God said to Moses, "I AM WHO I AM." And he said, "Say this to the people of Israel, 'I AM has sent me to you.'"

> God also said to Moses, "Say this to the people of Israel, 'The LORD, the God of your fathers, the God of Abraham, the God of Isaac, and the God of Jacob, has sent me to you.' This is my name forever, and thus I am to be remembered throughout all generations" (Exodus 3:13-15).

What Are Your Thoughts?

❀ What does this say about God and his personality? For your own walk in faith, what do you need to remember about the great I Am?

❀ In Psalm 48:12-14, we read that this is the legacy and the message the people of Zion are to pass along to the next generation:

> This is God, our God forever and ever.
> He will guide us forever (48:14).

❀ What does that message mean personally for you?

In Danger of Death

So Moses was persuaded to go back to Egypt and confront Pharaoh. He packed up his wife and family and started the journey, just like God told him to. But along the way, God did something else that was strange. As they stopped to settle down and rest for the night, God indicated that he was going to kill Moses (Exodus 4:24-26). I read this and thought, *What's going on here?* God had clearly commanded Moses to go and speak to Pharaoh, so it didn't make sense that now he wanted to kill his messenger.

While he lived in Midian, Moses must have taught his wife Zipporah about the Lord Jehovah, the Hebrew faith, and the Hebrew observances. We know this because Zipporah immediately knew why God threatened to kill Moses. She had that insight.

She knew Moses had neglected something very important. He had failed to circumcise his son. So right then and there, Zipporah did the job Moses should have: "Then Zipporah took a flint and cut off her son's foreskin and touched Moses' feet with it and said, 'Surely you are a bridegroom of blood to me!'" (Exodus 4:25).

She was mad! She was hot! Zipporah had a temper. And she was letting Moses know, "Don't you mess with my boy!" By her actions, Zipporah saved Moses and the Hebrew nation. Think about that!

And so they traveled on to Egypt. I'm sure you're familiar with the amazing story that's told in Exodus about Moses and Aaron's encounters with stubborn Pharaoh, and the plagues, the Passover, the death of all Egypt's firstborn sons, how Moses led the people of God out of Egypt in a hurry, how the Egyptians came after them, how the Israelites crossed through God's parting of the Red Sea, and how Pharaoh's army drowned when they tried to cross the sea.

Then God's people got stuck in the wilderness. And you know, it's so sad. They were only a two-weeks journey from the Promised Land, yet they had to stay 40 years in that wilderness because of their actions. They learned and experienced a great deal during that time.

Now shortly after the Israelites entered the wilderness a problem arose. Moses, their leader, was trying to take care of all the details and solve all the problems. He was the judge, the jury, the financier, the counselor, and more.

Jethro talked to Moses and advised him to delegate some of his duties to others, and it was all in God's providence. Delegation is needed because we all have been created and gifted for various purposes. None of us can be everything and do everything for everybody. We'll talk lots more about this later.

What Are Your Thoughts?

✲ What has God called you to and gifted you for during your life right now?

Our Only Hope

When we train up a child in the way he should go, when we look to God who is the author and the finisher of our faith, when we keep on living to see things turn around in our lives, this is when we're so blessed to know we have hope that's based on our heavenly Father who loves us so much. Yes, there was hope for the Israelites, and there is hope for me and you. Aren't you glad we have hope? I sure am!

Ultimately the only real hope for the world is Jesus Christ. The only help for the world is a touch from God, and that touch came to this world when Jesus stepped into it as our Savior and Lord. Think about our Savior's wonderful words in these passages:

> I am the door. If anyone enters by me, he will be saved and will go in and out and find pasture (John 10:9).

> I am the bread of life; whoever comes to me shall not hunger, and whoever believes in me shall never thirst (John 6:35).

> I am the way, and the truth, and the life. No one comes to the Father except through me (John 14:6).

What Are Your Thoughts?

✿ How do these passages confirm that Jesus is the world's only hope?

God Is in the Progressing Business

I'm telling you, I get so excited about Jesus and all he's done for me and you. I hope you're excited too! Think about the biblical truths you're learning and exploring. Make them an active part of your life, an active part of your character. And tell others about Jesus—your family and your friends. I hope you've gotten at least one thing out of this study so far that you want to tell somebody about. Then do it!

I like to say that God is in the *progressing* business. He's not into division and subtraction, but he's a part of addition and multiplication. He will add and multiply blessings to you when you're walking on his path and wearing whatever type of shoes the path you're on demands for today. Because God provides for me every day, I know he'll provide for you also. Let these passages confirm for you that God is in the progressing business!

> And we all, with unveiled face, beholding the glory of the Lord, are being transformed into the same image from one degree of glory to another. For this comes from the Lord who is the Spirit (2 Corinthians 3:18).

> So we do not lose heart. Though our outer self is wasting away, our inner self is being renewed day by day (2 Corinthians 4:16).

What Are Your Thoughts?

❀ What is your personal experience when it comes to hope and the other truths we've discussed so far? Express it in a word of praise for the work your God is accomplishing in your life day by day.

Yes, when we're on this journey, when we're walking in faith, then we're like the people whose situation is described so beautifully in Psalm 84:

> Blessed are those whose strength is in you,
>   in whose heart are the highways to Zion.
> As they go through the Valley of Baca [a dry region]
>   they make it a place of springs;
>   the early rain also covers it with pools.
> They go from strength to strength;
>   each one appears before God in Zion
>   (verses 5-7).

On this journey, we need never fear because we go *from strength to strength!* How is that possible? Because of this truth we acknowledge: "Our *strength* is in you, Lord!" And that means we can sing these words with David:

> I love you, O LORD, my strength.
> The LORD is my rock and my fortress and my deliverer,
> my God, my rock, in whom I take refuge,
> my shield, and the horn of my salvation, my stronghold
> (Psalm 18:1-2).

What Are Your Thoughts?

✿ As you walk in faith, as you go forward and take the next steps of *your* journey, in what specific ways will you need the Lord to be your strength, your rock, your fortress, your deliverer, your refuge, your shield, your horn of salvation, and your stronghold?

Let's Pray

> *Father God, you are so awesome! How we bow before you, how we bless your holy name, how we applaud you for giving us hope, and grace, and mercy. Thank you for helping us in our situations, for allowing us to walk through the things we walk through. Thank you that there is no incident, no situation, no circumstance in our future that you don't already know about.*
>
> *God, we ask you to touch us where we need it. Thank you for sharing the story of Moses to give us hope and strength as we use our ingenuity and knowledge about you to train up those who are young in the way they should go. Help us to be good examples to the people around us.*
>
> *As we continue this study, press into our hearts the truths that*

will help us to live better for you and to tell people about you and your kingdom. To you be the kingdom, and the power, and the glory forever.

O God, if we had ten thousand tongues, we couldn't thank you enough for all that you have done. Thank you especially for all that you have done for us in your Son, Jesus. How we love the name Jesus! How excellent is that name! How powerful is that name! And in his name we pray. Amen.

6

Exercising Faith to Conquer Your Fears

Before we move forward into Part 3 of this book, let's remember that faith is like a muscle—it takes exercise to build it up and keep it strong. So let's spend some together in this brief chapter looking into the Word of God to learn more about exercising our faith, especially in the face of fear.

I just have to say it again! Praise the Lord for giving us his Word to enjoy and examine and treasure in our hearts!

The Real Thing

Paul said that Timothy had "sincere faith" (2 Timothy 1:5). When it comes to faith, Timothy had the real thing.

What Are Your Thoughts?

❁ Do *you* have the real thing? How do you know that your faith is *sincere*?

Maybe the best way to check up on the reality and sincerity of your faith is simply to see how present and alive it is when you're facing fearful circumstances. Just two verses after the comment about Timothy's sincere faith, Paul gives him a reminder of his source of strength: "God gave us a spirit *not of fear* but of power and love and self-control" (2 Timothy 1:7). Sincere faith—the real thing—allows us to move *out* of fear and *in* to the experience of power and love and self-control. If we're still plagued by fears, then our faith isn't doing its job. Or rather, I should say that if fears have us in their grip, then our faith isn't yet strong and mature enough to do the job God means for it to do. Our faith has some more growing up to do.

What Are Your Thoughts?

❦ The disciples once said to the Lord, "Increase our faith!" (Luke 17:5). That's always a wise and healthy thing to ask for! Do you want bigger and better faith? Express your desire in a prayer to the Lord.

Faith That Needs to Grow

And how did Jesus respond to the disciples' request to increase their faith?

> And the Lord said, "If you had faith like a grain of mustard seed, you could say to this mulberry tree, 'Be uprooted and planted in the sea,' and it would obey you" (Luke 17:6).

Now what about that? Is the "amount" of faith required to accomplish the impossible—to bring about the miraculous—really only about the size of a poppy seed?

What Are Your Thoughts?

✻ What do *you* think Jesus meant by his "mustard seed" comment?

Jesus touched on this topic more thoroughly on a different occasion. A crowd had gathered, and a man came up to Jesus, fell to his knees, and said, "Lord, have mercy on my son, for he is an epileptic and he suffers terribly. For often he falls into the fire, and often into the water. And I brought him to your disciples, and they could not heal him" (Matthew 17:14-16).

In the midst of that crowd, with this distraught father kneeling before him, Jesus said, "O faithless and twisted generation, how long am I to be with you? How long am I to bear with you? Bring him here to me" (17:17). Then we read, "And Jesus rebuked the demon, and it came out of him, and the boy was healed instantly" (verse 18). This led later to further questioning from the disciples. They went to Jesus privately and asked, "Why could we not cast it out?" Jesus replied:

> *Because of your little faith.* For truly, I say to you, *if you have faith like a grain of mustard seed*, you will say to this mountain, "Move from here to there," and it will move, and nothing will be impossible for you (verses 19-20).

Jesus says there is such a thing as "little faith," and it's a kind of faith that's limited in what it can accomplish. The faith that can actually move a *mountain* is something different, something more—and yet it can be compared in size to the tiniest of seeds. In this instance or situation, what was Jesus wanting his disciples—and us—to better understand about faith? Was he indicating that it's not so much a matter of the size of our faith as it is the *quality* of it? Was he saying that if we have the *real thing*—the sincere faith that looks to Jesus—then it takes only a tiny bit of that to work miracles?

What Are Your Thoughts?

✿ What do you think Jesus is teaching us about faith in this situation? What does he want us to know and understand?

Small, Poor Faith

One thing is for sure. It was very important to Jesus that his disciples understand the truth about effective faith. Notice how often Jesus brought attention to the "smallness" of their faith:

> It happened when he was teaching them in the Sermon on the Mount and called their attention to the wildflowers on the hillside all around them: "If God so clothes the grass of the field, which today is alive and tomorrow is thrown into the oven, will he not much more clothe you, *O you of little faith?*" (Matthew 6:30).

> It happened again when they were together on a boat in the stormy Sea of Galilee and the disciples were afraid of drowning: "And he said to them, 'Why are you afraid, *O you of little faith?*' Then he rose and rebuked the winds and the sea, and there was a great calm" (Matthew 8:26).

> It happened again on the Sea of Galilee one night when Jesus walked to them on the water. At the Lord's invitation, Peter got out of the boat and walked on the water too…until he took his eyes off Jesus and began to sink. "Jesus immediately reached out his hand and took hold of him, saying to him, *'O you of little faith,* why did you doubt?'" (Matthew 14:31).

> It happened again when the disciples found themselves without food and anxious—even though Jesus had twice performed miracles of multiplying loaves and fishes to

feed huge crowds (and with plenty of leftovers!). So the Lord said to them, *"O you of little faith,* why are you discussing among yourselves the fact that you have no bread? Do you not yet perceive? Do you not remember the five loaves for the five thousand, and how many baskets you gathered? Or the seven loaves for the four thousand, and how many baskets you gathered?" (Matthew 16:8-10).

What Are Your Thoughts?

🕸 From your own experiences, what do you think "of little faith" might mean? Have you had times when your faith was feeble and deficient and low-quality? If so, what was that like?

🕸 When our faith is rich and full instead of poor and meager, Jesus says we're able to move a mountain (Matthew 17:20)! In what ways are your personal fears like a mountain that needs to be moved?

Mountains to Move

In Scripture, this imagery of mountains being eliminated or reduced goes back to the Old Testament. The prophet Isaiah spoke of "every mountain and hill...made low" (40:4), of mountains becoming a road (49:11), and of mountains departing and hills removed (54:10). The land of Israel has many hills and mountains, and the people of God could easily see how moving them away was beyond anyone's ability. If faith could move mountains, it was unquestionably powerful. Jesus used this picture often:

Have faith in God. Truly, I say to you, whoever says to this mountain, "Be taken up and thrown into the sea," and does not doubt in his heart, but believes that what he says will come to pass, it will be done for him. Therefore I tell you, whatever you ask in prayer, believe that you have received it, and it will be yours (Mark 11:22-24).

What Are Your Thoughts?

☘ What do the words of Jesus recorded in Mark 11 tell you about the power of faith?

◈ Specifically, what do those words of Jesus tell you about faith's connection with prayer?

☘ Look again at what Jesus said about faith and doubt. In your own words, explain the opposition and hostility between *faith* and *doubt*.

☘ How do you think *fear* is related to *doubt*?

☘ Perhaps the Holy Spirit has made you aware of some doubts you've been having in regard to what God can do or will do in your life. If that's true, how will you respond?

- I like these words of the great nineteenth-century English preacher Charles Spurgeon: "Be great believers! Little faith will bring your souls to heaven, but great faith will bring heaven to your souls." How does this encourage you?

In Paul's first letter to the Thessalonians, he told them he was praying "most earnestly night and day" that he could visit them face-to-face to "supply what is lacking in your faith" (1 Thessalonians 3:10).

What Are Your Thoughts?

- Do you think the Thessalonians were offended by Paul's statement? Do you think they might have felt he was belittling their faith?

Look how Paul commended the Thessalonians earlier in that letter:

> We give thanks to God always for all of you, constantly mentioning you in our prayers, remembering before our God and Father *your work of faith* and labor of love and steadfastness of hope in our Lord Jesus Christ…For not only has the word of the Lord sounded forth from you in Macedonia and Achaia, but *your faith* in God has gone forth everywhere, so that we need not say anything (1 Thessalonians 1:2-3,8).

What Are Your Thoughts?

- What do these words reveal about Paul's estimation of the faith of the Thessalonians?

❀ If he had such a positive view of the faith of the Thessalonians, what do you think he meant by saying their faith was "lacking"?

❀ Do you think the faith all believers have is lacking in one way or another? How about yours? Explain.

A Faith That's Bold

What Are Your Thoughts?

❀ Meditate on this incident with Jesus after his resurrection:

> Afterward he appeared to the eleven themselves as they were reclining at table, and he rebuked them for their *unbelief* and hardness of heart, because they had not *believed* those who saw him after he had risen (Mark 16:14).

❀ Why do you think Jesus responded to his disciples this way?

❀ In Ephesians 3:11-12, the apostle Paul shows us how it's "through our *faith*" in Christ Jesus our Lord that "we have boldness and access with confidence." Paul is speaking of access to God. What does this kind of boldness and access make possible in *your own experience of prayer?*

❀ Based on what you've studied so far about this topic, what does faith imply in regard to your *expectations*?

❀ The words of Jesus in John 14:1 are familiar to many of us, but I hope they never lose their wonder for us: "Let not your hearts be troubled. Believe in God; believe also in me." How does this form a direct attack on whatever fears you experience in your life as a believer?

❀ We find an equally wonderful message from the Lord just a few verses later: "Peace I leave with you; my peace I give to you. Not as the world gives do I give to you. Let not your hearts be troubled, neither let them be afraid" (John 14:27). What does the Lord want you to understand from these statements?

❀ Open your heart to these words: "Behold, God is my salvation; I will trust, and will not be afraid; for the Lord God is my strength and my song, and he has become my salvation" (Isaiah 12:2). How is the Lord God *your* salvation? What does that mean for you?

❀ How is the Lord God *your* strength? Again, what does that mean for you personally?

✿ How is the Lord God *your* song? How is this true for you?

✿ Think about the fears you face. How are those fears directly addressed by the fact that the Lord is *your* salvation, and *your* strength, and *your* song?

In Times of Trouble

The hardships and heartaches and hassles of life are recurring themes in life for all of us, aren't they? They make us nervous, anxious, and fearful even though we know God is worthy of our full trust. There is hope! As we keep growing in fuller, deeper awareness of why we can trust him, we'll be less fearful. Psalm 49 is a good one to turn to when times of trouble make us feel afraid—especially when other people are the source of that trouble:

> *Why should I fear in times of trouble,* when the iniquity of those who cheat me surrounds me, those who trust in their wealth and boast of the abundance of their riches? Truly no man can ransom another, or give to God the price of his life, for the ransom of their life is costly and can never suffice, that he should live on forever and never see the pit.
>
> For he sees that even the wise die; the fool and the stupid alike must perish and leave their wealth to others. Their graves are their homes forever, their dwelling places to all generations, though they called lands by their own names. Man in his pomp will not remain; he is like the beasts that perish.

This is the path of those who have foolish confidence; yet after them people approve of their boasts. Like sheep they are appointed for Sheol; death shall be their shepherd, and the upright shall rule over them in the morning. Their form shall be consumed in Sheol, with no place to dwell. But God will ransom my soul from the power of Sheol, for he will receive me (verses 5-15).

What Are Your Thoughts?

✿ What are the reasons given in Psalm 49 for *not being afraid?*

✿ In what ways does Psalm 49 foreshadow the great truths of the gospel of Jesus Christ?

✿ What lessons of *faith* are taught in Psalm 49?

You Have a Choice

When David says, "In the LORD I take refuge," he's telling us that he made the conscious choice to make the Lord his security (Psalm 11:1). David *takes* refuge in the Lord; it doesn't just happen.

What Are Your Thoughts?

✿ What does it mean to proactively *take refuge* in the Lord? What attitudes and actions do you think this requires from you?

In every part of Psalm 46, we find grounds for faith—and reasons to not be afraid:

> God is our refuge and strength, a very present help in trouble. Therefore we will not fear though the earth gives way, though the mountains be moved into the heart of the sea, though its waters roar and foam, though the mountains tremble at its swelling...
>
> Come, behold the works of the LORD, how he has brought desolations on the earth. He makes wars cease to the end of the earth; he breaks the bow and shatters the spear; he burns the chariots with fire. "Be still, and know that I am God. I will be exalted among the nations, I will be exalted in the earth!" (verses 1-3,8-10).

What Are Your Thoughts?

✿ In those verses from Psalm 46, what are the most important truth messages for building up your faith?

PART 3

Faith That Yields to God's Plans and Purposes

7

Wearing Grown-up Shoes

I get so fascinated when I'm writing to you and thinking about shoes. We've been exploring what it means to walk in faith on our journey through life. We've thought about the "shoes" we wear for that journey—shoes that can help us follow in the footsteps of faith and carry us down the path of righteousness.

When I graduated from high school in 1959 (I don't mind telling you how long ago it was!), I wore shoes with spike heels because I thought it was so cute. I wore them again for a while when I worked downtown at the beginning of my career.

I knew my great-grandparents had no money to send me to college, so I made the next best decision, and that was to go to secretarial school. I knew about such a school in downtown Dallas, and I called them up. The person I talked with said, "Come on down. We're registering right now." So I got on the streetcar. I had on this little-bitty blue dress with navy blue roses on it. I was wearing a belt around my little-bitty waist. And oh, honey, those high-heel shoes. Yeah, I was hot. And I was so excited because I was going to go to school and prepare for a career.

I got off the streetcar, and I walked across the street and went into the secretarial school. And the attitude definitely changed.

A man by the counter asked, "What are you doing here?"

I told him, "I came to enroll in school."

He said, "No you didn't."

I tried to explain what I'd just been told when I talked to someone on the telephone, but he took me by the arm and bodily thrust me out on the street. Well, needless to say, I was humiliated and embarrassed and angry. But I knew I could go home and tell on that man. I was sure Granny would take action.

Making a Way

So I went home and I told Granny what happened. And she said, "Baby, God will make a way."

Now that's *not* what I wanted to hear. I wanted to hear her say she was going right downtown to take that man on. But she didn't say that. She said, "Baby, God will make a way."

Then she called the lady she worked as a domestic for—Mrs. Mary Less. She told Mrs. Less that her great-grandbaby wanted to go to college.

Mrs. Less told Granny to have me come out to her home so she could talk to me in person. When I arrived she asked, "Where do you want to go to college?"

"North Texas State," I said.

Mrs. Less agreed to pay for my tuition and my books with two conditions: I couldn't let my grades fall below a C average, and I couldn't get married. "If you marry," she told me, "then you'll become your husband's responsibility" (remember, this was the 50s).

Well, that seemed fair enough.

I can do that, I thought.

And so Mrs. Mary Less did what she promised, and I did what I promised. What a blessing that lady was for me!

You see, my experience that day at the secretarial school was also a God setup, just like my being put in the closet at my grandmother's house. Had I been accepted into secretarial school, I might never have done the things that I've done. But that door was closed...and I thank God for closed doors! He has closed a lot of doors in my life. Some of them I've been mad about at the time, but sometimes we need doors closed in our faces to make us do something better. Do not despise closed doors! "Wait for the LORD; be strong, and let your heart take courage; wait for the LORD!" (Psalm 27:14).

Well, Mrs. Less did exactly what she said, and I went to school at North Texas State (now the University of North Texas). And then I got married. I've got to tell you that wonderful story!

God's Choice and Mine

As I've mentioned, I grew up in a house where people believed in prayer, they believed in reading and studying the Bible, and they were in church seven days a week. So I was taught to pray for everything I wanted—to ask God for *everything*. So at 12 years of age, I started praying for a husband. Now I didn't want him right then, mind you, but when the time came, I wanted my husband to be one that God selected.

In fact, I was taught that when it came to anything—even love— a person doesn't go out looking. God will send whatever it is. That's what I was taught.

So I started asking God to give me a good-looking husband, a smart husband, a kind husband, a husband with a good heart. I prayed for all those things because the men in my life—my granddaddy and my great-granddaddy—had shown me what to look for.

Fast-forward with me now to the time when I was 14. Something special happened. This boy came walking into Sunday school, and I thought, *That's the man I'm going to marry.* Now I was only 14. I wasn't allowed to talk to a boy on the telephone. I couldn't "take company." I couldn't date. I wasn't allowed to do anything like that. But what I could do was look at him in church. And he was so cute. Oh he was *so* cute.

And he kind of liked me too. I didn't flirt with him. I mean, I don't *think* I did. But maybe he thought I was. Finally, after some months had passed, I was able to talk with him on the phone. And then after a year or so, I was allowed to play Chinese checkers with him at my house, with my great-grandmother sitting there making sure no marbles fell on the floor, if you know what I mean. And then we were able to go out while chaperoned by my grandfather. And one day we were finally allowed to go out on a date—just the two of us.

Now my great-grandmother had stated outright that I could not be a teenage bride. So my twentieth birthday was on March 31, 1961, and I got married the very next day. Yes I did—on April Fool's Day! (Everybody remembers our wedding anniversary.)

George and I have been married nearly 50 years now. It hasn't all been wonderful; it hasn't all been peaches and cream. We've had our ups and downs. But we've had something greater than ups and downs. We've had the love of each other and we've had the Lord and his Word to guide us.

By the way, I found out later that George's uncle had told him there were two girls in the church who were wonderful and would make wonderful wives. And he mentioned my name and that of my friend Lynetta. So he wanted to meet both of us. But I met him first!

Today our marriage is stronger than ever. I couldn't travel and speak as I do now if I didn't have a man who was so supportive and confident of my ability and ministry. Being married to George is a privilege—a wonderful privilege.

A Promise Made Good

Meanwhile, you can guess what happened to my college education. Yes, I had to tell Mrs. Less I was getting married, and so that was the end of her financial support for my schooling. But my husband had promised my great-grandmother that he would make sure I completed my education after we were married. Wasn't that sweet of him? And he made good on that promise!

But let me tell you what *I* did. I was so much in love with him that one day I decided, *I'm too in love for an education.* I packed up my stuff at North Texas State University, loaded it into my friend's car, and she drove me back to Dallas. I announced to George, "I'm home!" I told him, "I'm not going back. I love you so much, I love you so much. *I love you so much!* And I can't stand being without you."

And he said, "Get your stuff back into my car. You're going back." I didn't even get to unpack.

All the way back to the school I didn't speak to him. I was too busy pouting. But now I thank God he insisted I finish my schooling. The fact that he had so much confidence in me and wanted the best for me was a blessing. And he continues to be quite a blessing.

Virtuous Woman

One time when my husband and I had a conflict, I started reading through Proverbs. I underlined everything the husband was supposed to do. Then I thought, *Well, maybe there's wisdom here for me too.* So I went back and highlighted everything the wife was supposed to do. And one of my highlights was the lengthy passage in Proverbs 31 about the godly wife. It starts like this:

> Who can find a virtuous wife? For her worth is far above rubies. The heart of her husband safely trusts her; so he will have no lack of gain (Proverbs 31:10-11 NKJV).

And it goes on to conclude this way: "A woman who fears the LORD, she shall be praised" (31:30 NKJV). If you read the full passage, you'll discover how this woman was not only wise and creative and hardworking, but she was also a woman of faith. Have you noticed that? "She considers a field and buys it; with the fruit of her hands she plants a vineyard" (verse 16). Actions like that take faith, don't they? And we read, "Strength and dignity are her clothing, and she laughs at the time to come" (verse 25). She can laugh at the time to come because of her faith in God's protection and provision.

What Are Your Thoughts?

❁ How about you? Can you "laugh at the time to come"? What does that mean to you?

I thank God that my husband's uncle shared with him that he thought I was a virtuous girl, and also for the fact that my husband consistently thinks of me that way.

A Virtuous Teenage Mother

When I think about the virtuous woman in Proverbs 31, I can't help but think about someone who was a virtuous woman even while she was still a teenager. In fact, she had a baby when she was probably 13 or 14 years old. I'm thinking about Mary and her first baby—Jesus, the Messiah, Emmanuel, *God with us*. Do you remember that when the angel Gabriel went to Mary to tell her she was going to conceive a child, it was perplexing to her? She didn't know how this could be so he explained it:

> And Mary said to the angel, "How will this be, since I am a virgin?"
>
> And the angel answered her, "The Holy Spirit will come upon you, and the power of the Most High will over-shadow you; therefore the child to be born will be called holy—the Son of God" (Luke 1:34-35).

What Mary was being asked to do was by no means easy. That's why I so appreciate her response: "And Mary said, 'Behold, I am the servant of the Lord; let it be to me according to your word'" (Luke 1:38).

One of the most powerful attributes of a virtuous woman is to hear God's Word and follow his instructions. Mary yielded herself to God's plan and purpose. That's what it means to be "the servant of the Lord," which is the beautiful way she described herself.

What Are Your Thoughts?

❀ Do you want to refer to yourself as "a servant of the Lord"? What does that phrase mean to you?

❀ *Serving God* is a main theme in the Scriptures, and it's a large part of walking in faith. Write down what these verses say about being a servant of the Lord.

Serve the Lord with gladness! Come into his presence
with singing! (Psalm 100:2).

[Jesus said,] "Blessed are those servants whom the master
finds awake when he comes. Truly, I say to you, he will
dress himself for service and have them recline at table,
and he will come and serve them" (Luke 12:37).

[Jesus said,] "If anyone serves me, he must follow me;
and where I am, there will my servant be also. If anyone serves me, the Father will honor him" (John 12:26).

Now we are released from the law, having died to that
which held us captive, so that we serve not under the old
written code but in the new life of the Spirit (Romans
7:6).

[The apostle Paul said,] "For am I now seeking the
approval of man, or of God? Or am I trying to please
man? If I were still trying to please man, I would not be
a servant of Christ" (Galatians 1:10).

How much more will the blood of Christ, who through

the eternal Spirit offered himself without blemish to God, purify our conscience from dead works to serve the living God (Hebrews 9:14).

Therefore they are before the throne of God, and serve him day and night in his temple; and he who sits on the throne will shelter them with his presence (Revelation 7:15).

❧ Now that you've looked at those Scriptures, why does it take *faith* to be a true servant of the Lord?

8

Hearing and Trusting

Before I met my husband, while I was still a teenager praying for the best husband someday, I made a special request to God. I said, "God, when the man I'm going to marry shows up on the scene, let everything be clean in my house on the same day." Now that sounds really strange, doesn't it? But the fact is, we didn't do all our housecleaning on one day. We scattered it out throughout the week. So to have absolutely everything clean at the same time was not a normal occurrence. So I threw that "fleece" or test out, asking God to show me. (If you don't know about Gideon and the fleece, check out Judges 6:36-40.)

Sure enough, years later, there was a time when my great-grandmother and I did all our housecleaning in one day—washing and scrubbing floors and all the rest. We even went to the beauty shop and got prettied up ourselves. It was the only day like it that I can ever remember. And though at the moment I didn't recall my "fleece," God later brought it to my memory. Yes, it was the same day I saw George for the first time. Yes, I knew he was the one. I had no doubt about it then, and I have no doubt today. He's my God-intended husband. I was made for him, and he was made for me. And that's in spite of the fact that sometimes we get on each other's nerves. Yes, we do, and that's the truth.

And you may think the sign I requested—about everything being clean on the same day—was a serious prayer. But for God to answer that prayer of mine was nothing compared with how mysterious and amazing it was for him to send Gabriel with that announcement to Mary that she was going to give birth to the Messiah. We can honor Mary, the most virtuous woman and the only woman ever to conceive a child without knowing a man, as long as we remember she was a woman—and totally human. She wasn't perfect. However, she was the only woman whom the Spirit of God overshadowed so that she gave birth to a child who would grow and become the only Man/God who could redeem mankind by dying for us, conquering death and hell and the grave for us, and then arising on the third day to give us victory.

Mary's Faith

What did Mary do to demonstrate her faith? One huge thing she did was to sing her praise to the Lord when she visited her relative Elizabeth. We find her song of praise in Luke 1:46-55. Listen to the way Mary's faith rings out from these words—a faith that was obviously rooted in knowing God's truth revealed in the Old Testament Scriptures:

> My soul magnifies the Lord,
> and my spirit rejoices in God my Savior,
> for he has looked on the humble estate of his servant.
> For behold, from now on all generations will call me blessed;
> for he who is mighty has done great things for me,
> and holy is his name.
> And his mercy is for those who fear him
> from generation to generation.
> He has shown strength with his arm;
> he has scattered the proud in the thoughts of their hearts;
> he has brought down the mighty from their thrones
> and exalted those of humble estate;
> he has filled the hungry with good things,
> and the rich he has sent away empty.
> He has helped his servant Israel,

in remembrance of his mercy,
as he spoke to our fathers,
to Abraham and to his offspring forever
(Luke 1:46-55).

What Are Your Thoughts?

🏶 From the words of this song, what is Mary trusting God for?

🏵 Also from the words of her song, what are the biggest truths that Mary clearly believes about her God?

🏵 What words in Mary's song are true for *you* in your relationship with your heavenly Father?

Hearing from God

Not long ago a woman asked me, "How do you know when God is speaking to you? I think he speaks to me, but I'm not sure." God has spoken to me many times, and in all my experiences, I've never heard him speak audibly. What I do sense is a still small voice speaking inside me. So how do I know it's him? Because I have absolute peace. And I mean *absolute* peace—not a little bit of peace, not a wondering peace, not a "well, was it him?" peace. No, I have *total peace* in my mind and in my heart.

A few years ago I was pursuing a certain business situation, and I wanted to approach it from God's perspective. Within ten days I was supposed to offer a full response to the people I was dealing with, and I was asking God to help me figure out what to do. I was relating to him in an advisory capacity. Have you ever done that? Have you ever tried to advise God? He doesn't take our advice too well, does he?

As I was trying to figure out this business issue, I went away to our house in the country and said, "God, I'm going to stay here seven days. I'm going to fast and pray, and I know you're going to give me everything I want so I can deal with these people the way you want me to."

On my first day I was fasting and praying, and listening—but I heard nothing from God.

The second day, I fasted and prayed again. "God," I told him, "I've got my pencil and paper ready. I really want to hear from you, okay?"

I heard nothing. N-O-T-H-I-N-G, *no* thing.

And on the third day...nothing.

By then I was reminding God, "I came down here for a purpose. Would you please answer my prayer?"

And on the fourth day I heard, "Trust me."

I got out my pencil and paper 'cause then I knew he was about to lay out for me exactly how I was to trust him and everything this would involve. I sat there...and I heard nothing more.

Trusting Him

On days five, six, and seven, I heard God speaking only this sound bite: "Trust me." Wow!

But after that seventh day, I had such peace in my spirit. I packed up and drove back to Dallas. In regard to that business issue, I told myself, "I'm not going to do one thing." I didn't call them, and they didn't call me—for eight months!

I didn't do a thing because God said, "Trust me." I had total peace about that. And then after eight months, I heard God tell me, "Call them."

I wondered what was I going to say to them, but I sensed God indicating he would speak for me.

So I called the people and told them what I needed. I asked them to send me a signed copy of the agreement by three o'clock the next day.

Their answer? "Okay."

You see, if I hadn't been obedient to God, if I hadn't listened to him eight months earlier, if I hadn't accepted his sound bite, I'm sure I would have messed up the whole thing.

Listening and Faith

Who can find a virtuous woman—a woman who will listen to God, who will confide in God? A woman who will be protected by God, and who will tell other people the story about how God has helped her in her situations? A woman who will trust him until she dies?

That's the kind of woman I want to be!

Are the ears of your heart tuned in to listen to the Lord?

God longs so deeply for his people to listen to him. Look at the argument and the plea he makes about this in Psalm 81:8-16:

> Hear, O my people, while I admonish you!
>> O Israel, if you would but listen to me!
> There shall be no strange god among you;
>> you shall not bow down to a foreign god.
> I am the LORD your God,
>> who brought you up out of the land of Egypt.
>> Open your mouth wide, and I will fill it.
> But my people did not listen to my voice;
>> Israel would not submit to me.
> So I gave them over to their stubborn hearts,
>> to follow their own counsels.
> Oh, that my people would listen to me,
>> that Israel would walk in my ways!
> I would soon subdue their enemies
>> and turn my hand against their foes.
> Those who hate the Lord would cringe
>> toward him,
>> and their fate would last forever.
> But he would feed you with the finest
>> of the wheat,
>> and with honey from the rock I would satisfy you.

What Are Your Thoughts?

❦ From what you see of God's heart for you (and all his people) in those words from Psalm 81, why is it so important for you to listen carefully to him?

> Faith comes from hearing, and hearing through the word of Christ (Romans 10:17).

Your faith can't help but grow when you listen attentively and obediently to the Word of God.

I Will Trust

In my church we sing:

> I will trust in the Lord.
> I will trust in the Lord.
> I will trust in the Lord until I die, oh yes.

And when we sing that, we know what we're saying. That's why I can tell God, "*I'm ready to walk in faith!* I've lived long enough, I've experienced enough, I've seen enough that now I'm just going to relinquish what I have to you."

That's what Mary was doing when she said to God's messenger, "I am the servant of the Lord; let it be to me according to your word" (Luke 1:38). I hope you can say that too. I hope you can say, "God, whatever situation I'm in, whatever shoes I'm walking in, whatever terrain I'm walking on—whether it's rocky or it's soggy or quicksand—*God, I'm ready to walk in faith with you.*" If you can say that, then I encourage you to live it out. Enjoy that privilege and that adventure!

Being virtuous like the Proverbs 31 woman doesn't mean you won't make mistakes. But it does mean you'll learn to recognize the mistake, you'll repent of the mistake, and you'll move on. You won't hold on to it, and you won't let it hold on to you. (As one of my friends says, "Guilt is the gift that keeps on giving.") You'll move forward, and you'll also be able to show other people how to walk in the faith God has given them.

Yes, you and I have had many sorrows and cried many tears. We wonder about tomorrow. But as believers in and followers of Jesus Christ, we know who holds our tomorrow. We don't have to worry about what's going on or what isn't going on, we don't have to worry about the uncertainties in this world. We don't have to worry about any of that because, as virtuous women, our integrity, strength, intelligence, ingenuity, and righteousness bear witness to God's values and his kingdom.

Let's teach our children and the people around us how to be virtuous and full of faith like Mary was.

Let's Pray

Lord God, we so appreciate that you're our God and our Father. You are so wonderful to us! You've given us everything in your Book so that we can be virtuous and walk in your ways. How delighted we are that you provided this as the basis to live. And you've given us your Word to share with other people so they can discover who you are too. Thank you!

Father, as we continue to study the walk of faith, give us clarity in our minds to see what you want us to see in your Scriptures. You've told us how to deal with conflict, you've told us how to deal with grief, and you've shown us how to deal with finances. And you have helped us understand how we need to trust you with all our hearts. Help us not lean on our own understanding. In all our ways we want to acknowledge you and allow you to direct our paths.

Father, speak to our spirits and let us know you love us, you care for us, you hold us, and you protect us even when we're walking through hardships.

We ask all this in Jesus' name. Amen.

9

Exercising Faith to Accept God's Higher Plans and Purposes

I hope you're gaining confidence in declaring, "Lord, I'm ready to walk by faith!" I know I am. As we keep stepping forward, and as we get ready to move into Part 4 of this book, let's get some more help from the Word of God about exercising our faith. We're going to focus especially on strengthening our faith so that we can more quickly accept God's higher plans and purposes for our lives—especially when we're not happy with the direction our lives seem to be going.

I believe that we sometimes forget how crucially important our faith is to God. Let's explore this together.

What Are Your Thoughts?

❈ The apostle Jude gave us this prompting: "Now I want to remind you, although you once fully knew it, that Jesus, who saved a people out of the land of Egypt, afterward destroyed those who did not *believe*" (Jude 5). In your own words, what does this verse tell you about the importance of faith?

✿ The apostle Paul stated his personal desire and intention to be "found" in Christ, possessing not his own righteousness "but that which comes through *faith* in Christ, the righteousness from God that depends on *faith*" (Philippians 3:9). In your own words, explain what this verse tells you about faith's importance.

✿ Notice these words from the apostle James:

> If any of you lacks wisdom, let him ask God, who gives generously to all without reproach, and it will be given him. But let him ask in faith, with no doubting, for the one who doubts is like a wave of the sea that is driven and tossed by the wind. For that person must not suppose that he will receive anything from the Lord; he is a double-minded man, unstable in all his ways (James 1:5-8).

❀ In your own words, what does this passage say to you about the importance of faith?

❀ From this passage, how is faith connected with *wisdom* and *stability* in your life?

✿ The apostle John wrote:

> Whoever *believes* in the Son of God has the testimony in himself. Whoever *does not believe* God has made

him a liar, because he *has not believed* in the testimony
that God has borne concerning his Son. And this is
the testimony, that God gave us eternal life, and this
life is in his Son. Whoever has the Son has life; whoever does not have the Son of God does not have life
(1 John 5:10-12).

✿ According to the truth and the authority of those words, what
do you see as the importance of faith?

Guarded and Protected

The apostle Peter also teaches us a great deal about the great worth
and value of our faith.

What Are Your Thoughts?

❇ In 1 Peter 1:5, Peter tells us that "by God's power" we "are being
guarded through faith for a salvation ready to be revealed in the last
time." Our faith *guards and protects* us all along our life's way, ensur-
ing that we enter eternity with the One in whom we believe. What
do you see as the greatest dangers that you need to be guarded and
protected *from* in this life?

❇ After bringing up the subject of "various trials" that bring grief to
our lives, Peter goes on to mention "the tested genuineness of your
faith" (1 Peter 6-7). He says that this genuineness is "more precious
than gold that perishes though it is tested by fire." In what ways—
through what trials—has *your* faith been tested and proven to be
genuine?

❀ And someday—hallelujah!—this proven genuineness will "result in praise and glory and honor at the revelation of Jesus Christ" (1 Peter 1:7). Our faith in the Lord is never in vain!

✖ Peter goes on to talk about "the outcome of your faith, the salvation of your souls" (verse 9). Why is this such a precious and wonderful "outcome" to you?

✖ A few verses later, Peter focuses again on faith. In a rich and profound statement, he reminds us that it's because of "the precious blood of Christ" that we "are *believers* in God, who raised him from the dead and gave him glory, so that your *faith* and hope are in God" (verses 19 and 21). Why is it important to remember the link between our faith and the death of Christ *and* the resurrection of Christ?

❀ Reflect also on this passage from Paul: "If Christ has not been raised, then our preaching is in vain and your *faith* is in vain... And if Christ has not been raised, your faith is futile and you are still in your sins" (1 Corinthians 15:14,17). What does this tell you about how much your faith depends on the resurrection of Christ?

After urging us onward in 1 Peter to greater love and respect for one another (1:22; 2:1), Peter mentions our faith again as he paints a picture of a wonderful new temple—a "spiritual house" that all of God's people are being built into "as living stones" (2:5). In that new holy temple, Jesus is the foundation and cornerstone. Then Peter brings in faith by quoting from the book of Isaiah:

> For it stands in Scripture: "Behold, I am laying in Zion a stone, a cornerstone chosen and precious, and whoever *believes* in him will not be put to shame" (2:6).

This belief in Christ, Peter says, is an *honor:*

> So the *honor* is for you who *believe*, but for those who do not believe, "The stone that the builders rejected has become the cornerstone," and "A stone of stumbling, and a rock of offense." They stumble because they disobey the word, as they were destined to do (1 Peter 2:7-8).

What Are Your Thoughts?

❀ What is Peter trying to get you to understand about the importance of your faith?

Deep Roots

Real faith means being *rooted.* In the parable of the sower and the seeds, Jesus told how some seed "fell on the rock, and as it grew up, it withered away, because it had no moisture" (Luke 8:6). He went on to explain: "And the ones on the rock are those who, when they hear the word, receive it with joy. But these *have no root;* they *believe* for a while, and in time of testing fall away" (verse 13). The faith these people have is not a *lasting* faith; it's not a *durable* faith because it is not a *deeply rooted or fixed* faith.

What Are Your Thoughts?

✿ How would you describe the *roots* of your faith? What are they drawing nourishment from? How long have they been doing this? Are they well-established? Are they rooted mostly in rocky ground or in good soil? Write your answer as extensively as you can. Don't hold back from examining your faith.

✿ With a sense of urgency and high purpose, Paul said to the believers in Corinth (and us): "Examine yourselves, to see whether you are in the faith. Test yourselves" (2 Corinthians 13:5). What do you think such an assessment should involve? What kind of questions should you ask to test and examine your faith?

✿ Through the prophet Isaiah, the Lord tells us, "If you are not firm in faith, you will not be firm at all" (Isaiah 7:9). Why is your *faith* so important to the stability and consistency of your life?

✿ Paul teaches us about our need to "continue in the faith, stable and steadfast" and to be "established in the faith" (Colossians 1:23; 2:7). What are the most important things God has done in your life to stabilize you in your faith?

From Doubt to Faith

Without intending to, the "doubting" apostle, Thomas, gave us a lasting lesson on faith after the resurrection of Jesus. Do you remember the story? The disciples were together in an upper room in Jerusalem after the crucifixion when Jesus suddenly entered, stood among them, spoke to them, and ministered to them. However, "Thomas, one of the Twelve, called the Twin, was not with them when Jesus came. So the other disciples told him, 'We have seen the Lord.' But he said to them, 'Unless I see in his hands the mark of the nails, and place my finger into the mark of the nails, and place my hand into his side, *I will never believe*'" (John 20:24-25).

What Are Your Thoughts?

✿ In this situation, what limitations was Thomas placing on his faith?

⊛ Do you ever place similar limitations on your faith? Do you place other limitations on your faith?

Let's finish the story:

Eight days later, his disciples were inside again, and Thomas was with them. Although the doors were locked, Jesus came and stood among them and said, "Peace be with you." Then he said to Thomas, "Put your finger here, and see my hands; and put out your hand, and place it in my side. Do not disbelieve, but believe."

Thomas answered him, "My Lord and my God!"

Jesus said to him, "Have you believed because you have seen me? Blessed are those who have not seen and yet have believed" (John 20:26-29).

✽ What do you think is included in the blessing that belongs to all people who believe in the resurrected Jesus even though they haven't seen him?

✽ What do you think Thomas learned from this situation? What effect do you think it had on his faith?

Adding On to Faith

Did you know that in God's eyes, your faith has the same status as the faith of the apostles? Peter tells us about this in the opening lines of his second letter:

> Simeon Peter, a servant and apostle of Jesus Christ, to those who have obtained *a faith of equal standing with ours* by the righteousness of our God and Savior Jesus Christ (2 Peter 1:1).

What Are Your Thoughts?

✽ According to that passage, what gives your faith an equal rank with the faith of Peter and the other apostles?

In this second letter, Peter goes on to outline a program or process, so to speak, for increasing and strengthening and multiplying our faith. First he reminds us of some incomparably wonderful truths: the "divine power" that's available to us, the divine "glory and excellence" we've been called to, and God's "precious and very great promises" that allow us to escape "from the corruption that is in the world because of sinful desire" (2 Peter 1:3-4). Then he shows us where to take our faith—how we are to build on the *foundation* of faith:

> For this very reason, make every effort to supplement your faith with virtue, and virtue with knowledge, and knowledge with self-control, and self-control with stead-fastness, and steadfastness with godliness, and godliness with brotherly affection, and brotherly affection with love (1:5-7).

What Are Your Thoughts?

❈ In your own words, describe those qualities Peter mentions that you are to build on as the foundation of your faith.

Next Peter tells us why the qualities on his list are so important:

> For if these qualities are yours and are increasing, they keep you from being ineffective or unfruitful in the knowledge of our Lord Jesus Christ. For whoever lacks these qualities is so nearsighted that he is blind, having forgotten that he was cleansed from his former sins. Therefore, brothers, be all the more diligent to make your calling and election sure, for if you practice these qualities you will never fall. For in this way there will be richly provided for you an entrance into the eternal kingdom of our Lord and Savior Jesus Christ (2 Peter 1:5-11).

What Are Your Thoughts?

❀ Based on what Peter tells us (in 2 Peter 1:8-11), how would you express in your own words the importance of these qualities that God wants us to add to our faith?

❀ As you reflect on these things that Peter told us in 2 Peter 1:3-11, ask, "How does all this relate to my understanding of God's higher plans and purposes for my life?" Write down the connections you see.

❀ Now choose *one* quality on Peter's list. Focus on it, meditate on it, and write down how you can strengthen it in your life.

A Higher Purpose—and Higher Promises

Paul tells Timothy (and us!) that God "saved us and called us to a holy calling, not because of our works but because of his own purpose and grace, which he gave us in Christ Jesus before the ages began" (2 Timothy 1:9).

What Are Your Thoughts?

❀ When you think about God's purposes for your life, what major truth do you find in Paul's words to Timothy? What is significant about God's purpose for you?

You may struggle with understanding God's big-picture purpose for your life. We all do—and quite often. But a big part of that picture is made clear in the promises he gives us, promises that outline what he intends our lives to become. And those promises are given to us to receive and embrace with faith.

Remember Peter's description of God's promises? They are "precious and very great" (2 Peter 1:4), and because of what they are and what they do, Peter tells us to keep growing our faith by developing and nurturing our positive character qualities, which we discussed earlier. Now let's think more about those "precious and very great promises."

Charles Spurgeon, the great English preacher of the nineteenth century, wrote a book exploring the promises of God. He called it *Faith's Checkbook* and explains the title this way:

> A promise from God may very instructively be compared to a check payable to order. It is given to the believer with the view of bestowing upon him some good thing. It is not meant that he should read it over comfortably, and then have done with it. No, he is to treat the promise as a reality, as a man treats a check.
>
> He is to take the promise, and endorse it with his own name by personally receiving it as true. He is by faith to accept it as his own. He sets to his seal that God is true, and true as to this particular word of promise. He goes further, and believes that he has the blessing in having the sure promise of it, and therefore he puts his name to it to testify to the receipt of the blessing.
>
> This done, he must believingly present the promise to the Lord, as a man presents a check at the counter of the Bank. He must plead it by prayer, expecting to have it fulfilled. If he has come to Heaven's bank at the right date, he will receive the promised amount at once. If the date should happen to be further on, he must patiently wait till its arrival; but meanwhile he may count the promise

as money, for the Bank is sure to pay when the due time arrives.

Some fail to place the endorsement of faith upon the check, and so they get nothing; and others are slack in presenting it, and these also receive nothing. This is not the fault of the promise, but of those who do not act with it in a common-sense, business-like manner.

God has given no pledge which He will not redeem, and encouraged no hope which He will not fulfill…

The sight of the promises themselves is good for the eyes of faith: the more we study the words of grace, the more grace shall we derive from the words.

What Are Your Thoughts?

✽ Have you learned to embrace God's promises in the way Spurgeon did? Which of the promises are you most consciously claiming and praying these days? List as many as you can.

Faith and Knowing

Faith is like knowing, and faith *brings* knowing. The apostle John said, "I write these things to you who *believe* in the name of the Son of God that you may *know* that you have eternal life" (1 John 5:13).

What Are Your Thoughts?

✽ What do you really believe about Jesus? What are the most important things you *know* with absolute certainty about Jesus?

❀ Now go back and put numbers by each one, ranking them in order of personal meaningfulness to you.

The *knowing* that comes with faith influences our actions:

> And by this we know that we have come to *know* him, if we keep his commandments (1 John 2:3).
>
> We *know* that we have passed out of death into life, because we love the brothers (1 John 3:14).

❀ The *knowing* that comes with faith brings love for others and holy obedience. What have you come to truly *know* about God, yourself, and others because of your growing faith in Jesus Christ?

❀ What are the most important spiritual realities that you *know* will be true in your life once you reach eternity and are in the direct presence of the Lord?

❀ What are the most important spiritual realities that you long to be more evident in your life before you leave this world?

The Dangers of Doubt, Disbelief, and Disobedience

The writer of the book of Hebrews emphasizes the dangers of lacking faith. Harkening back to examples of rebellious doubt and disobedience by the people in Old Testament times when God's people wandered in the wilderness, he quotes Psalm 95 as he tells us,

Therefore, as the Holy Spirit says, "Today, if you hear his voice, do not harden your hearts as in the rebellion, on the day of testing in the wilderness, where your fathers put me to the test and saw my works for forty years. Therefore I was provoked with that generation, and said, 'They always go astray in their heart; they have not known my ways.' As I swore in my wrath, 'They shall not enter my rest'" (Hebrews 3:7-11).

What Are Your Thoughts?

✸ In what ways do you see lack of faith as being a "hardening of the heart"?

✸ We're told to specifically *not* harden our hearts. How do we keep our hearts from hardening?

The passage in Hebrews continues:

Take care, brothers, lest there be in any of you an evil, unbelieving heart, leading you to fall away from the living God (3:12).

What Are Your Thoughts?

✸ From God's perspective, why is an "unbelieving heart" evil?

Hebrews 3:13-14 points us to something we need to hold on to:

> Exhort one another every day, as long as it is called "today," that none of you may be hardened by the deceitfulness of sin. For we share in Christ, if indeed we hold our original confidence firm to the end.

What Are Your Thoughts?

✿ Our *faith* is "our original confidence," and that's what we're to hold "firm to the end." In your life, what do you expect will be the biggest threats to this?

The writer of Hebrews then takes a closer look at the Old Testament examples of those who lost their faith:

> As it is said, "Today, if you hear his voice, do not harden your hearts as in the rebellion." For who were those who heard and yet rebelled? Was it not all those who left Egypt led by Moses? And with whom was he provoked for forty years? Was it not with those who sinned, whose bodies fell in the wilderness? And to whom did he swear that they would not enter his rest, but to those who were disobedient? So we see that they were unable to enter because of unbelief (3:15-19).

What Are Your Thoughts?

✿ What was the result of the people's unbelief?

✿ What warning does that carry for you and me?

> Therefore, while the promise of entering his rest still
> stands, let us fear lest any of you should seem to have
> failed to reach it. For good news came to us just as
> to them, but the message they heard did not bene-
> fit them, because they were not united by faith with
> those who listened (4:1-2).

The message we hear from God must be united by faith with the hearers of that message. *Faith* is what makes God's message stick. The same is true for us today in regard to the Good News of Jesus Christ.

What Are Your Thoughts?

✿ In what ways has the gospel been united with your life?

PART 4

Faith That Succeeds

10

Wearing Bling-bling Shoes

I have some shoes with little bling-bling bumblebees on them. I love those shoes. They're unique, they're colorful, and they flash! To me, bling-bling says I'm the cat's meow. Somebody asked me not long ago, "Did you buy those like that or did you put those bees on there?" My answer? I'm not all that clever. I bought them that way.

Now, even apart from their flash, those bumblebees have deep significance to me. Let me tell you the story behind my bumblebee obsession and some of the events and happenings that propelled me to where I am today—ministering God's truths to people all across the United States and even into some other countries.

Ever since I started school in the first grade, my life has been reinvented by God every 12 years. How do I know that?

I was lying in bed one night thinking, and as I was thinking, I started counting. And I recognized the tremendous changes that had come into my life in 1960 (when I graduated from high school), and in 1972, and then 1984, and 1996, and the 2008. *Wow, 12—the number of authority, the number of judgment,* I thought. Every 12 years God has given me a different assignment. And sometimes the next assignment is more difficult than the previous one. For example, the 1960 transition was pretty momentous.

My Banking Job

In the 1960s I'd become a wife and a mother, and yet sometimes in those years I didn't really know who in the world I was. I wondered, *Who am I? Where am I? Why am I? Am I?* I decided I needed to get out of the house and get a job. Okay, actually my doctor told me to find a job because I was going through depression. One of his remedies was for me to find work outside my home and to stop living so introspectively. So I did.

I worked as a substitute teacher for a while in the community where I lived, and that was great. Yet I didn't feel this was my life's vocational calling. I prayed, "God, I really want to work at North Park National Bank." That was where my husband and I had our bank accounts, and it was right near our home. Working there would be so convenient! I didn't know a thing about banking, but I knew I could learn.

After praying, I called the human resources person there—a Mr. Newman. I told him, "I'm going to work for your bank, and I have my résumé ready to give to you. Would you please meet me in the bank lobby?"

He said, "Ma'am, the bank is already closed."

And I said, "Yes, I know, it's after three. Meet me in the lobby of the bank, please." (That was back when banker hours were nine o'clock to three o'clock.)

I look back on my forwardness now and think, *Girl, you were a mess!* But I convinced him to meet me in the lobby, and I handed him my résumé. He said they weren't hiring, but for the next several months I called him once a week. "Are you ready to have someone interview me yet?" And I reminded him, "I'm going to work for your bank."

Finally he wouldn't accept my calls. But that was all right. I showed up at his office. His secretary said, "I'm sorry, he's busy." And I said, "That's okay, I can sit here. I have nothing else to do."

To make a long story short, the bank finally hired me!

Something's Wrong

It wasn't long before I sensed that nobody in the banking industry knew a lot about how it worked. I came to that conclusion because when I asked people the same question I always got different answers. *There's something wrong with this picture,* I decided.

After my probationary period, which I passed with flying colors, I told my bosses, "I need to go to banking school, and I'm sure y'all will send me." So they sent me to the American Institute of Banking. I was soon certified in a number of different areas. Then I said to Judy, my friend and the CEO of the American Institute of Banking, "I want to *teach* banking."

She said, "What?"

"I want to teach banking."

"You don't know anything about banking."

"That's why I want to teach it. Nobody else knows anything either. Maybe we'll learn together."

"Okay," she said. "I'll try you out one semester." That job ended up lasting 15 years!

As I was teaching bank professionals and officers—people who had plenty of experience already, I noticed most of them had low self-esteem. They would get frightened when I'd say the word "test," or "quiz," or "homework." They were petrified.

So I prayed. "God, will you give me something I can say to these people that will encourage and influence and empower them to be the best they can be?"

Then one day when I was going into our church building, my friend, who happens to be a lot more animated than I am, came up to me. "Thelma Wells!" she exclaimed. "That *suuuuure* is a pretty bee! And every *tiiiiime* you wear that bee, remember! You can *beeeeeee* the best at what you want to be!" I was wearing a little jeweled pin in the shape of a bee, which when I put it on that morning had no particular significance to me except it was pretty.

But my friend had planted a seed—a seed from God, I'm sure.

As I started thinking about bees, I remembered that I'd read about them...that aerodynamically, the bumblebee isn't supposed to be able to fly. Its body is too heavy; its wingspan is too shallow. But the fool thing doesn't know it can't fly, so it flies—doing what God created it to do!

I was fascinated. So I started talking about the bumblebee. I quickly adopted the bumblebee as my metaphor for life and made it my special logo. Next I developed a little program around B + E + E = S. I call it "a formula for success." Not *the* formula for success—because that's Jesus. He's the ultimate formula for success. But B + E + E = S is *a* formula for success. I started talking about this on the last nights of the banking courses I taught. Soon people were asking me if I would come and talk about this topic to their organization or club or church. And I said yes. So I was soon sharing what God had laid on my heart as a metaphor for my life. And as I did, I would "dissect" the bee for them. In fact, let me do that for you now, okay?

"B"

"B" is for *Be aware of who you are.* What is your mission? What is your vision? What is your passion? Why were you born? Many people haven't figured any of them out. And maybe you haven't either. If you haven't, don't worry. I was 40 years old before I figured it out. And then I discovered I was already doing what I enjoyed doing—and that it was my calling.

If you say, "I don't know why I'm here," then I say to you, "What do you *like* doing? If it's what you like doing it, that's probably your calling (as long as it's legal)." And remember that while you're figuring these things out, you shouldn't be comparing yourself to anybody. You are an individual created for a specific purpose. Remember Psalm 139? We can acknowledge before God the same truth David did: "You formed my inward parts; you knitted me together in my mother's womb. I praise you, for I am fearfully and wonderfully made" (Psalm 139:13-14).

You are unique. How wonderful that is! You don't even have the same toe print or fingerprint as anyone else. God wants to remind us, "You don't have to look like or act like anybody else because I made you an individual the way I wanted you to be. And I love diversity!"

What Are Your Thoughts?

❧ Express in writing what your mission and vision are for your life.

Share your passion, your calling, why you are where you are, and why you were born. If you're not sure, just start writing and perhaps God will bring it to your mind. Answer as fully as you can.

✿ No matter how clear (or unclear) this is to you, be sure to pray about it thoroughly. Why not include Psalm 57:2 in your prayer? "I cry out to [you,] God Most High, to [you] God who fulfills [your] purpose for me."

❀ In prayer, tell God you need help understanding your purpose in life. Ask for his wisdom and guidance. Thank him for making you in a unique way, with a unique calling, with a unique purpose.

"E"

The first "E" means *Eliminate the negatives.* Or, better said, "Eliminate the effects of negativity in your life." All of us face negativity. We encounter disappointments and heartache and we face hardships and trials.

What Are Your Thoughts?

✿ What negative influences tend to have the most impact in your life today?

How can we eliminate or at least minimize the effects of all that negativity? At the knees of my great-grandmother, I learned that our first and best response to everything is to pray. Did I hear you say you're not sure how to pray? Let me assure you, if you can talk and think, you can pray. In fact, you don't even have to know how to express your deepest feelings. Sometimes a good prayer is just a moan or a groan 'cause the Holy Spirit can interpret that groan and intercede for you. The Word of God says, "The Spirit himself intercedes for us with groanings too deep for words" (Romans 8:26).

So pray.

Yes, there may be times when you've told yourself, "I don't feel like praying," or "I'm too tired to pray," or "God, I prayed last week about that, and you didn't answer." When you don't feel like praying or just don't want to pray, I suggest that you *sing!* Praise God through song. You might not be able to sing as well as others, but you can make a joyful noise! And go to the Bible for inspiration. There are wonderful songs of praise in the Bible! Express yourself with the love and hope God gives you. We need to do these things because God rejoices over those who joyfully praise him. In Zephaniah 3:14, he says, "Sing aloud, O daughter of Zion; shout, O Israel! Rejoice and exult with all your heart, O daughter of Jerusalem!" Then he goes on to say, "The LORD your God is in your midst, a mighty one who will save; he will rejoice over you with gladness; he will quiet you by his love; he will exult over you with loud singing" (verse 17). When we rejoice in him, he rejoices in us.

Back in my childhood days when I was locked in the closet, I sang the church hymns I knew. God accepted my innocent praise. And when I've done something wrong, God still accepts my contrite prayers and beckons me to draw closer to him. So I know he will accept your praise wherever you are, whatever you've done, however you've acted. Your God-pleasing praise will help you walk in faith and counter the effects of negativity.

What Are Your Thoughts?

❧ Read the following passages that highlight praising God. Write down your heart response to each one. While you're writing, dedicate your thoughts to God and remember that your praise pleases and honors him.

I will give to the LORD the thanks due to his righteousness, and I will sing praise to the name of the LORD, the Most High (Psalm 7:17).

I will give thanks to the LORD with my whole heart; I will recount all of your wonderful deeds. I will be glad and exult in you; I will sing praise to your name, O Most High (Psalm 9:1-2).

You have turned for me my mourning into dancing; you have loosed my sackcloth and clothed me with gladness, that my glory may sing your praise and not be silent. O LORD my God, I will give thanks to you forever! (Psalm 30:11-12).

I will bless the LORD at all times; his praise shall continually be in my mouth. My soul makes its boast in the LORD; let the humble hear and be glad. Oh, magnify the LORD with me, and let us exalt his name together! (Psalm 34:1-3).

I will sing to the LORD as long as I live; I will sing praise to my God while I have being (Psalm 104:33).

Praise the LORD! I will give thanks to the LORD with my whole heart, in the company of the upright, in the congregation (Psalm 111:1).

I will extol you, my God and King, and bless your name forever and ever. Every day I will bless you and praise your name forever and ever (Psalm 145:1-2).

❀ Why is *praise* to the Lord so important for building up our faith?

When you're facing negative pressures or uncertainty about something, I recommend that you talk to somebody you trust, somebody who will draw on the Word of God in his or her counsel instead of his or her own opinion. Quite frankly, opinion doesn't count much.

I have a spiritual accountability person, and every time I get hung up on something, I call Debra. Sometimes Debra gets on my nerves because she seldom offers a quick answer or solution. Instead she says, "Let me check with God on that." And then she gets back with me.

I'm always appreciative, though, because I can know she won't lead me astray. She'll point me to the path of righteousness.

What Are Your Thoughts?

✿ What friend(s) do you have who will help you by being a worthy spiritual accountability partner?

"E"

The second E in B + E + E = S is all about *eternal value*. What does this mean in a nutshell? *Only what you do for Christ will last.* Yes, we can get involved in a lot of stuff, but if what we do isn't for the cause of Christ and the kingdom of God, it's going to fade away. For instance, if I'm working for people's accolades, and I allow myself to get pumped up by that, I have my reward—and it's not eternal.

What Are Your Thoughts?

✿ What about you? Are you working for the kingdom of God? Do you have an eternal perspective? Explain.

✿ Engage your heart and mind with the following passages. Write down what each one teaches you about eternal value and eternal perspective. If you're familiar with some of the verses, reflect on it patiently in case the Holy Spirit wants to show you something new.

> You make known to me the path of life; in your presence there is fullness of joy; at your right hand are pleasures forevermore (Psalm 16:11).

> As for me, I shall behold your face in righteousness; when

I awake, I shall be satisfied with your likeness (Psalm 17:15).

Whom have I in heaven but you? And there is nothing on earth that I desire besides you. My flesh and my heart may fail, but God is the strength of my heart and my portion forever (Psalm 73:25-26).

Do not lay up for yourselves treasures on earth, where moth and rust destroy and where thieves break in and steal, but lay up for yourselves treasures in heaven, where neither moth nor rust destroys and where thieves do not break in and steal. For where your treasure is, there your heart will be also (Matthew 6:19-21).

For this slight momentary affliction is preparing for us an eternal weight of glory beyond all comparison, as we look not to the things that are seen but to the things that are unseen. For the things that are seen are transient, but the things that are unseen are eternal (2 Corinthians 4:17-18).

But our citizenship is in heaven, and from it we await a Savior, the Lord Jesus Christ, who will transform our lowly body to be like his glorious body, by the power that enables him even to subject all things to himself (Philippians 3:20-21).

If then you have been raised with Christ, seek the things
that are above, where Christ is, seated at the right hand
of God. Set your minds on things that are above, not on
things that are on earth. For you have died, and your life
is hidden with Christ in God. When Christ who is your
life appears, then you also will appear with him in glory
(Colossians 3:1-4).

"S"

Finally, the "S" stands for *success*. Everybody wants success; everybody's looking for it. I love what Booker T. Washington said: "Success is
to be measured not so much by the position that one has reached in life
as by the obstacles which he has had to overcome while trying to succeed."

What Are Your Thoughts?

🎀 How do you define success?

Meditate on the following passages and write down what they have
to do with true success.

[Jesus said,] "In the world you will have tribulation. But
take heart; I have overcome the world" (John 16:33).

Who shall separate us from the love of Christ? Shall tribulation, or distress, or persecution, or famine, or naked-
ness, or danger, or sword?...No, in all these things we
are more than conquerors through him who loved us
(Romans 8:35,37).

Do not be overcome by evil, but overcome evil with good (Romans 12:21).

[Paul said,] "I can do all things through him who strengthens me" (Philippians 4:13).

You are strong, and the word of God abides in you, and you have overcome the evil one (1 John 2:14).

Everyone who has been born of God overcomes the world. And this is the victory that has overcome the world—our faith. Who is it that overcomes the world except the one who believes that Jesus is the Son of God? (1 John 5:4-5).

✿ Take an especially close look at the following success messages from Jesus. What is your heart's response to each one? What is Jesus asking of you, and what is he promising you?

To the one who conquers I will grant to eat of the tree of life, which is in the paradise of God (Revelation 2:7).

The one who conquers will not be hurt by the second death (2:11).

To the one who conquers I will give some of the hidden manna, and I will give him a white stone, with a new name written on the stone that no one knows except the one who receives it (2:17).

The one who conquers and who keeps my works until the end, to him I will give authority over the nations (2:26).

The one who conquers will be clothed thus in white garments, and I will never blot his name out of the book of life. I will confess his name before my Father and before his angels (3:5).

The one who conquers, I will make him a pillar in the temple of my God. Never shall he go out of it, and I will write on him the name of my God, and the name of the city of my God, the new Jerusalem, which comes down from my God out of heaven, and my own new name (3:12).

The one who conquers, I will grant him to sit with me on my throne, as I also conquered and sat down with my Father on his throne (Revelation 3:21).

11

Beautiful in Every Way

The B + E + E = S formula reminds me of a beautiful woman mentioned in the Old Testament. Her name is Esther. If you've read her story, I'm sure she's someone you like and admire. Let's review what we know about her.

Early in the book of Esther, we read how Persia's King Ahasuerus (also known as Xerxes) decided to exile his queen, who had not been as dutifully submissive as the king and his advisors wanted her to be. (The men were afraid other women would follow her example.) Therefore the king decreed that the empire's most beautiful girls be brought to him so he could choose a replacement to Vashti. Among the beautiful young women brought in was Esther, an orphan who was being raised by her cousin Mordecai. Esther and the other "candidates" went through a year of beauty treatments. (Except for the reason, can you imagine how nice it would be to be pampered for an entire year?)

During this time, the king's right-hand official, Haman, was filled with fury because Mordecai refused to bow down and pay homage to him as the king had commanded (Esther 2:5). But Haman "disdained to lay hands on Mordecai alone," so he used his influence with the king to set up a plan to destroy *every* Jew in the kingdom.

Esther and the Bees

Now let's look at Esther in light of B + E + E = S. Esther knew who she was. She knew she was Jewish. She'd been told by Mordecai, however, not to reveal this for the right time had not yet come. Esther also knew she was attractive. Because she was beautiful inside and out and true to herself, she obtained favor in the sight of all who knew her.

The Truth About Us

You're attractive too, especially in God's eyes, and that's the truth. Do you accept that truth about you? Do you ever try to be somebody else? All of us at one time or another have played "let's pretend" to hide something about ourselves. But God created you to be you—the person you really are.

Once I was writing a book, and it was taking me a long time—going on two years. I couldn't understand why; I'd written and finished other books in far less time. So I called the person I was supposed to turn the manuscript in to. I said, "I am *not* writing this book. I hate this book." I had even moved the computer files of my work onto a disk, and I didn't care if that disk burned up or got lost. I just wasn't going to finish that onerous job.

But the person I was talking with said, "You really need to pray about this."

"I have *been* praying, and I am *not* writing the book."

And the person said, "No, *really pray* about this."

"Okay, but I can tell you right now, I'm not writing it," I said stubbornly. I did pray about it though: "God, do you want this book written? If you do, then help me write it." Around three o'clock one morning God woke me up. He spoke to me as he always does—through my spirit. He said, "Write the book like you talk. Stop trying to be somebody else."

You see, I'd read all these other books by wonderful authors, and I'd picked out something I liked from one author, and something else I liked from another, and this and that from still others, and I tried to reproduce all that in my book. So it was shaping up to be nothing from me. That wasn't God's best for me or for the book. And it was making the entire process almost impossible. So I had to learn, just like Esther did, to be myself.

What Are Your Thoughts?

❀ In what ways have you had to learn to just be yourself?

Esther's Situation Gets More Dire

Esther also learned how to eliminate the negatives. She prayed about her situation. In fact, she went beyond praying. She included fasting, and she asked others to fast with her. That's what she focused on as she faced the next great crisis.

Let's take a closer look.

> When Mordecai learned all that had been done, Mordecai tore his clothes and put on sackcloth and ashes, and went out into the midst of the city, and he cried out with a loud and bitter cry (Esther 4:1)

Meanwhile, all the Jews throughout the kingdom learned about their danger. "And in every province…there was great mourning among the Jews, with fasting and weeping and lamenting, and many of them lay in sackcloth and ashes" (4:3).

When Esther heard about Mordecai's public mourning she was "deeply distressed" (4:4). She sent a message to find out what was the matter, and Mordecai sent a message back to let her know about the deadly trouble Haman had started.

To most of us it would seem obvious what Esther would do. In her privileged position as the queen, she would use her influence on the king in this urgent matter. So we might suppose Esther would send a message to Mordecai saying, "Oh, I'll just have a little talk with the king about it. We'll get this straightened out." But it wasn't that easy. In fact, that approach wasn't even *possible*. Everybody knew the rules for approaching the king, but Esther reminds Mordecai of them: "If any man or woman goes to the king inside the inner court without being called, there is but one law—to be put to death." There was only one exception: "The one to whom the king holds out the golden scepter... may live" (4:11).

It had been a month since Esther had been asked to be in the king's presence. Before she was asked to see him again, the killing of the Jews might have already started.

While Esther thought about what to do, Mordecai sent her a sobering reminder: "Do not think to yourself that in the king's palace you will escape any more than all the other Jews. For if you keep silent at this time, relief and deliverance will rise for the Jews from another place, but you and your father's house will perish" (verse 14).

Mordecai had enough faith in God to know that ultimately God's people would survive. But he was also realistic enough to realize that many Jews would die, possibly including them. Mordecai closed this latest message to Esther with an intriguing, throat-gulping thought: "And who knows whether you have not come to the kingdom for such a time as this?" (verse 14). He was essentially saying, "Yes, the situation is as grim as can possibly be. The hour is gravely desperate. *But you, Esther, just happen to be queen at this moment. This is your moment to act!*"

Esther sent this reply to her kinsman Mordecai: "Go, gather all the Jews to be found in Susa, and hold a fast on my behalf, and do not eat or drink for three days, night or day. I and my young women will also fast as you do. Then I will go to the king, though it is against the law, and if I perish, I perish" (4:16).

How brave she is! Esther's courage is the kind that *faith* makes possible. In this terrible crisis, Esther knew that the same God who had allowed circumstances that made her queen could also miraculously use her to influence the king and rescue his people. And that's exactly what he did! Esther's faith was rewarded. The Jews were saved, Mordecai was promoted to second in rank to the king, and Haman was put to death.

How Does Esther's Story Encourage Us?

Are you facing a crisis? Are you dealing with great difficulties? Are you walking through something you don't know how to get out of? Do you feel like you're walking in quicksand or drowning in a flood? Are you dealing with something that makes you feel lonely and afraid?

Queen Esther shows us that fasting and praying to God is the best way to approach God and ask him to intercede and help us. Other books of the Bible also encourage us to pray and fast: 2 Samuel 12:23; 2 Chronicles 20:3; Matthew 6:16; and Luke 5:34 to name a few.

Let's look at Isaiah 58:1-12, where the Lord talks to us about true fasting, and the kind of things it should lead to in our lives. This will help us deal with the negatives in our lives too. God says he isn't satisfied by the kind of fasting that only causes a person to humble himself with a bowed head. The kind of fasting God seeks always extends to much more:

> Is not this the fast that I choose: to loose the bonds of wickedness, to undo the straps of the yoke, to let the oppressed go free, and to break every yoke?
>
> Is it not to share your bread with the hungry and bring the homeless poor into your house; when you see the naked, to cover him, and not to hide yourself from your own flesh?
>
> Then shall your light break forth like the dawn, and your healing shall spring up speedily; your righteousness shall go before you; the glory of the LORD shall be your rear guard.
>
> Then you shall call, and the LORD will answer; you shall cry, and he will say, "Here I am." If you take away the yoke from your midst, the pointing of the finger, and speaking wickedness, if you pour yourself out for the hungry and satisfy the desire of the afflicted, then shall your light rise in the darkness and your gloom be as the noonday.

And the LORD will guide you continually and satisfy your desire in scorched places and make your bones strong; and you shall be like a watered garden, like a spring of water, whose waters do not fail. And your ancient ruins shall be rebuilt; you shall raise up the foundations of many generations; you shall be called the repairer of the breach, the restorer of streets to dwell in (Isaiah 58:6-12).

What Are Your Thoughts?

✿ What specific kinds of actions does God seek from his people, according to Isaiah 58:6-12?

 ✿ What do these things reveal about God's values and standards for our dealings with other people?

 ✿ When we apply these things to our own time and culture, what kinds of actions on our part would be in obedience to what God asks for in this passage?

✿ What promises does God make to his people in Isaiah 58:6-12?

 ✿ What would the fulfillment of those promises look like if God carried them out among us today?

Willing to Sacrifice

Esther was willing to sacrifice her life for her people. She committed herself to go and speak to the king at great peril. She said, "If I perish, I perish" (Esther 4:16).

What Are Your Thoughts?

❀ What kind of courageous actions is God asking you to make at this time or in this season of your life?

Standing before the king, Esther finally revealed her identity as a Jew, thus risking her life again. She knew in her heart this was something she had to do for the kingdom. She did all this because she was thinking not only in terms of immediacy but also in terms of *eternal value*.

And because Esther walked forward in faith, came before the king so boldly yet with tact and respect, revealed her heritage, and was obedient to Jehovah God, the plot against the Jews was countered by allowing the Jews to defend themselves. The Jews were saved, Haman was killed, Mordecai was honored, and Esther was a powerful influence in the kingdom.

Gullibility and Grace

I have a confession to make. I've been known to take faith at face value, humanly speaking. Someone passes along something for me that they say God told them to tell me, and being the trusting person I am, on occasion I don't consult God myself about it. I just lean on the other person's understanding.

Last year I was told by someone that God told her to do something out of the ordinary for me. With tears in her eyes and a trembling in her voice and convincing body language, she shared her plans. I listened to this news with awe-filled surprise. I just knew this had to be a message from God to me because it was in line with something he had already prompted me to do. The only thing I didn't know was when he wanted me to do it.

So I believed this person. We proceeded with plans to do what this person said God had told her. The plans for the project seemed to be working out superbly, but there was a gnawing in my spirit that I couldn't figure out.

When the time was near for the project to be presented, the Spirit of God moved me to check into the availability of what was promised. When I did, I was given the assurance that things were working the way God had said.

Even then I didn't consult with God for his confirmation. I was trusting and standing on the woman's understanding and interpretation of what God had told her. I assumed the promises the person said came from God really did. It was blind faith for sure.

The project went extremely well, and everyone involved benefited greatly. I so wish that had been the finale. But no. Several months later it became clear that the person couldn't fulfill the financial obligation as promised. This left me in a financial bind and the possibility of tarnishing my business reputation.

I had so many questions. Had God led me this far to leave me? Didn't God know what was going to happen? Why didn't God blow his trumpet more loudly in my ear and tell me not to get involved with this person? And what was I to do now? I did much soul-searching and inquiring of God (finally!). Instead of relying on someone else's hearing God's plans for me, I relied on him directly.

It's amazing how God gives guidance and clarity when we truly call on him and rely on him for directions. I was obedient and did exactly what he prompted me to do about the situation. I trusted in him to cover this situation with his amazing grace and bountiful mercy. I thanked him for allowing me to go through this season even in the midst of my trusting in a human being instead of him. I praised him for his mercy because he helped me even though I didn't go to him for my original marching orders on the project.

As I communicated with the Lord, I knew he would bring about the right conclusion. I was so calm that people who knew about the situation were surprised. The people on the business end were baffled because they knew what was happening. I had not perpetrated this mess. I had not purposefully planned it. I had not deliberately deceived anyone. But I had walked in the shoes of gullibility. I did step into the muck and mire of questionable integrity. And I stumbled and fell into a financial cave that seemed to have no exit.

Nevertheless, in spite of my failure to "seek the LORD while he may be found" and to wait for his instructions for the project, and despite my taking what the person said at face value, and regardless of my vulnerability and fleshly excitement about what was promised, God stepped in and saved the day. He made sure I was not a victim.

So what did I learn from this? That sometimes we fail to really wait on the Lord because we're too busy pursuing the success we want. I learned that some people who come bearing promises and gifts based on "a word from the Lord" may not know what they're talking about or may not be telling the truth. I relearned the hard way that my trust should never be in what a human says or does. I was reminded that I should always verify and confirm with God what I am to do.

I was reassured that I can trust God to see me through or get me out of situations when I unknowingly dive into water that's too fierce to swim in alone.

Sweet friend, I hope you will learn from my error. Be assured that God knows our intentions because he knows the desires and thoughts of our hearts. He knows we're imperfect and need him to help us in *all* our ways. God knows the way we're going to go and has already planned a means of escape when we get off course. Sometimes that exit cuts straight through the problem, sometimes it's going around the situation, and sometimes it's staying in the circumstances and seeing it through.

Because of the awesome covering of God, we can always say, "Thank you, Lord! Thank you, Lord! Oh thank you, Lord!"

I'm not saying we'll never get off course, but I am saying that now we know that when someone tells us something is "from the Lord," we need to reply, "Thank you for sharing that. Let me seek God's confirmation and guidance on that before we move forward." And when I respond this way, I always add, "If God plans this for us, he'll also make it clear to me."

And did you notice that even in the midst of that project God let me know in my spirit that something wasn't quite right? Isn't it wonderful that he'll do that for us? He will give us sweet peace about the situation or trouble our souls until we pay attention. This is what it means to fully walk by faith and not by sight.

Second Corinthians 4:18 says, "We look not to the things that are seen but to the things that are unseen. For the things that are seen are transient, but the things that are unseen are eternal." Our eyes may cause us to consider paths that weren't designed for us, but the footprints of Jesus will guide us in the straight path of righteousness if we are paying attention.

In Christ You Can BEE the Best!

My favorite advice to people is, "Don't take my word for anything!" Go to the book—God's book—the Bible. That's the ultimate source for God's wisdom and guidance. This is the book that tells you how to trust God. That's what he wants us to do. He wants us to be able to sing with joy this wonderful song by Reverend William C. Martin (1864–1914):

> I trust in God wherever I may be,
> Upon the land or on the rolling sea,
> For, come what may, from day to day,
> My heav'nly Father watches over me.
> I trust in God, I know He cares for me,
> On mountain bleak or on the stormy sea;
> Tho' billows roll, He keeps my soul,
> My heav'nly Father watches over me.

Trust in God! He tells us over and over throughout the Bible that he loves us and he cares about us. And he wants you to be the very best at who he created you to be!

And this brings me back to my motto! "*In Christ* you can BEE the best!"

When I was working in corporate America, I would say to people, "You can be the best of what you *want* to be." And sometimes when I said that, I sensed a check in my spirit from the Lord. I prayed for God to give me boldness—boldness in the presence of the corporations and government agencies and educational institutions that I worked with. I specifically prayed, "God, give me boldness for you because I am trusting in you." And after that infusion of boldness from God my words changed. At the end of all the courses I taught from that point on, after I had presented telephone skills, or customer service skills, or leadership skills, or whatever it was, I would say, "Now there's one more thing I have to say to you, and I want you to listen to me carefully. For me, I believe that none of these skills really work until you know Jesus."

I could see the astonishment in the attendees' faces. "She said 'Jesus!'" "Yes, I did!" I wanted to shout. And because of obedience to God's command to be who I am, to be who he created me to be, there's only one of me in the whole world (hallelujah for that!). And I have to say something about Jesus!

Yes, it's *in Christ* that you can BEE the best.

In Christ

Have you ever gone through the New Testament epistles and looked for all the "in Christ" statements. That will be one of the richest and most encouraging word studies you can do! Here are a few of those passages I came across when I did that word study. I hope you will reflect on each one, especially thinking how each one relates to *true success for you in God's eyes*. Will you do that? And to help you in your reflection, be sure to write down your thoughts.

What Are Your Thoughts?

✿ Write down your heart-responses to these "in Christ" statements.

> There is therefore now no condemnation for those who are *in Christ Jesus* (Romans 8:1).

If anyone is *in Christ*, he is a new creation. The old has passed away; behold, the new has come (2 Corinthians 5:17).

In him we have redemption through his blood, the forgiveness of our trespasses, according to the riches of his grace (Ephesians 1:7).

For we are his workmanship, created *in Christ Jesus* for good works, which God prepared beforehand, that we should walk in them (Ephesians 2:10).

My God will supply every need of yours according to his riches in glory *in Christ Jesus* (Philippians 4:19).

Therefore, as you received Christ Jesus the Lord, so walk *in him*, rooted and built up *in him* and established in the faith, just as you were taught, abounding in thanksgiving (Colossians 2:6-7).

Give thanks in all circumstances; for this is the will of God *in Christ Jesus* for you (1 Thessalonians 5:18).

Let's Pray

> *O God, you are the author and finisher of our faith—and also of our success. You bring success to us, and you put it in our hearts and in our minds to obey you and to follow your ways to attain that success. Thank you for Esther and for preserving her story for us so we can better understand that we've been sent here for such a time as this to carry out our work for your kingdom. What a privilege that is for us!*

> *Whatever situations we're walking into, whatever we're going through, we ask that you prepare us and remind us that you will work all things together for good for those who love you. Thank you for sending the Holy Spirit to help us. He helps us eliminate the negatives and look to you instead of getting locked into introspection. In Jesus' name. Amen and amen!*

12

Exercising Faith for Your Success

We've been exploring how active faith takes attentive effort, active faith takes work, *active faith takes exercise*. Before we go on to Part 5, let's discover God's gracious help for us in building our faith for success—success as *he* defines it.

Do you know the beautiful description in the very first psalm? "Blessed is the man...[whose] delight is in the law of the LORD, and on his law he meditates day and night." God ensures that such a person is *successful:* "He is like a tree planted by streams of water that yields its fruit in its season, and its leaf does not wither. *In all that he does, he prospers*" (verse 3). That person prospers in *every endeavor God leads him into* because his faith is like the leaves on that stream-side tree and his good works are like the tree's fruit.

The apostle James describes faith: [Abraham's] *"faith was active along with his works, and faith was completed by his works"* (James 2:22). Industrious faith, diligent faith, get-your-hands-dirty faith is what makes faith all it can be—that *completes* it.

What's the most intense kind of "work" our faith should be busily involved in? I believe the answer to that question is in Paul's words in Galatians 5:6: "For in Christ Jesus neither circumcision nor uncircumcision counts for anything, but only *faith working through love*." *Love* puts faith to work.

What Are Your Thoughts?

❦ In what relationships does God want you to put your faith to work right now? What will that mean and look like in each relationship?

Recognizable Faith

Real, vibrant faith is something so active and substantial people can *see* it. This is revealed in an incident involving the apostle Paul and Barnabas on their first missionary journey:

> Now at Lystra there was a man sitting who could not use his feet. He was crippled from birth and had never walked. He listened to Paul speaking. And Paul, looking intently at him and *seeing that he had faith to be made well*, said in a loud voice, "Stand upright on your feet." And he sprang up and began walking (Acts 14:8-10).

What Are Your Thoughts?

❦ Now imagine that you were Barnabas standing there with Paul when this happened. What about this crippled man would indicate to you and Paul that he had the "faith to be made well"?

Yes, faith can be visibly recognizable. Do you remember the time when a paralytic man was lowered through the roof by his four friends so he could be touched by Jesus and healed? It's in the second chapter of Mark.

The scene was a crowded house in the town of Capernaum. "And many were gathered together, so that there was no more room, not even at the door. And [Jesus] was preaching the word to them" (verse 2). "And they came, bringing to him a paralytic carried by four men."

Suddenly there was a commotion overhead and dust and debris probably floated down. "And when they could not get near him because of the crowd, they removed the roof above him, and when they had made an opening, they let down the bed on which the paralytic lay" (verses 3-4).

The next verse is the one I want to draw your attention to: "When Jesus saw their faith, he said to the paralytic, 'Son, your sins are forgiven'" (verse 5)!

Jesus *saw* their faith! If you and I had been there, we might have seen something else and missed the faith entirely. We might have seen a rude interruption. We might have seen an outlandish or humorous or dangerous or inconsiderate action. But a lesson in faith—a *demonstration* of faith? Would we have caught that? I'm not sure. But Jesus did!

Think about those four friends of that paralytic man. Isn't it wonderful that he had friends like that? Four friends who *believed* in Jesus enough to go to all that trouble to place their friend at his feet?

What Are Your Thoughts?

❁ Let me ask a question that may be a little uncomfortable for you but it's important for your spiritual health. What about *your* faith is *visible?* What aspects of your faith can people see? What kind of activities, what kind of movements, what kind of demonstrations are in plain sight?

And let's not forget the rest of the story about the paralytic man. It shows us so clearly how the *faith* in Jesus that brought healing for this paralyzed man is the same *faith* that brings us forgiveness for our sins.

> Now some of the scribes were sitting there, questioning in their hearts, "Why does this man speak like that? He is blaspheming! Who can forgive sins but God alone?"
>
> And immediately Jesus, perceiving in his spirit that they thus questioned within themselves, said to them, "Why do you question these things in your hearts? Which is easier, to say to the paralytic, 'Your sins are forgiven,' or to say, 'Rise, take up your bed and walk'? But that you may know that the Son of Man has authority on earth to forgive sins"—he said to the paralytic—"I say to you, rise, pick up your bed, and go home."
>
> And he rose and immediately picked up his bed and went out before them all, so that they were all amazed and glorified God, saying, "We never saw anything like this!" (Mark 2:6-12).

Attention-grabbing Faith

Let's think some more about this kind of faith that gets God's attention. Do you remember the story about the faith of a man who sought healing from Jesus for his dying servant? It's found in Luke 7:1-10.

> Now a centurion had a servant who was sick and at the point of death, who was highly valued by him. When the centurion heard about Jesus, he sent to him elders of the Jews, asking him to come and heal his servant. And when they came to Jesus, they pleaded with him earnestly, saying, "He is worthy to have you do this for him, for he loves our nation, and he is the one who built us our synagogue."
>
> And Jesus went with them. When he was not far from the

house, the centurion sent friends, saying to him, "Lord, do not trouble yourself, for I am not worthy to have you come under my roof. Therefore I did not presume to come to you. But say the word, and let my servant be healed. For I too am a man set under authority, with soldiers under me: and I say to one, 'Go,' and he goes; and to another, 'Come,' and he comes; and to my servant, 'Do this,' and he does it."

When Jesus heard these things, he marveled at him, and turning to the crowd that followed him, said, "I tell you, not even in Israel have I found such faith." And when those who had been sent returned to the house, they found the servant well.

"Such faith!" Jesus exclaimed. Here's the kind of faith that should really grab our attention. It certainly grabbed Jesus'!

What Are Your Thoughts?

❀ As you think about your successes, how do these promises from the Lord relate to you? Explain why they are relevant.

Good and upright is the LORD; therefore he instructs sinners in the way. He leads the humble in what is right, and teaches the humble his way...Who is the man who fears the LORD? Him will he instruct in the way that he should choose (Psalm 25:8-9,12)—

Thus says the LORD, your Redeemer, the Holy One of Israel: "I am the LORD your God, who teaches you to profit, who leads you in the way you should go" (Isaiah 48:17)—

I cry out to God Most High, to God who fulfills his purpose for me (Psalm 57:2)—

The LORD will fulfill his purpose for me; your steadfast
love, O LORD, endures forever. Do not forsake the work
of your hands (Psalm 138:8)—

And I am sure of this, that he who began a good work in
you will bring it to completion at the day of Jesus Christ
(Philippians 1:6)—

Keys for Success

God's Word provides a lot of keys for success, so we'll just look at
a few.

What Are Your Thoughts?

🕮 What key for success is found in the following passage? What does
it mean for *you?*

> Now may the God of peace who brought again from the
> dead our Lord Jesus, the great shepherd of the sheep, by the
> blood of the eternal covenant, equip you with everything
> good that you may do his will, working in us that which
> is pleasing in his sight, through Jesus Christ, to whom be
> glory forever and ever. Amen (Hebrews 13:20-21).

❀ And what key for success is found in this passage? What does it
mean for *you?*

> Now may the God of peace himself sanctify you com-
> pletely, and may your whole spirit and soul and body be
> kept blameless at the coming of our Lord Jesus Christ.
> He who calls you is faithful; he will surely do it (1 Thes-
> salonians 5:23-24).

❀ Again, what key for success is found in the following passage? And
how does it relate to *you?*

> Now may our Lord Jesus Christ himself, and God our
> Father, who loved us and gave us eternal comfort and
> good hope through grace, comfort your hearts and estab-
> lish them in every good work and word (2 Thessalonians
> 2:16-17).

❀ Now that you've studied the keys to success a bit more, what do you
think *success* for *you* means from God's perspective?

❀ In what ways will your *faith* be required to attain this success?

What Faith Can Accomplish

What Are Your Thoughts?

❀ What do each of these passages tell you about what faith can accomplish?

> And the prayer of faith will save the one who is sick, and the Lord will raise him up. And if he has committed sins, he will be forgiven (James 5:15)—

> And these signs will accompany those who believe: in my name they will cast out demons; they will speak in new tongues; they will pick up serpents with their hands; and if they drink any deadly poison, it will not hurt them; they will lay their hands on the sick, and they will recover (Mark 16:17-18)—

❀ What encouragement toward stronger faith do you find in these words from the apostle John?

> And this is the confidence that we have toward him, that if we ask anything according to his will he hears us. And if we know that he hears us in whatever we ask, we know that we have the requests that we have asked of him (1 John 5:14-15).

PART 5

Faith That Fights

13

Wearing Combat Boots

Do you feel like you're having to fight for something all the time? For your family, for your health, for your financial security? Are you thinking you might as well put on combat boots for this journey through life, even though they'll probably hurt your feet after a while? Is there heavy, *heavy* combat out on your battlefield?

Maybe it seems that the shoes you've been wearing into life's battles are all tattered and torn and worn out. You feel unprotected and unprepared for the battles you face.

Family Battle

I'm in a battle right now for my family—and it's a battle that has been going on for three decades. It's not my whole family that's in a crisis, but the entire family is affected when one family member is out of kilter. Everybody suffers; everyone feels repercussions.

I have three children: two daughters who have loved the Lord with all their hearts for a long while and a son who is struggling. He has accepted Christ, but sometimes young men feel the need to prove their manhood in counterproductive ways, don't they?

For years we've encountered negative circumstances because of decisions my son and/or his friends have made. We've watched situations unfold that we knew weren't God's best. We're sure God did not design or order them. But I know God can fix the problems. I know he will welcome my son into a closer relationship with him whenever my son wants it.

But even knowing all this, the question that comes up in my mind is, *Why hasn't God stepped in, taken care of things, and brought my son back into alignment with him?* I am persuaded that because God knows everything about everybody, in every situation, that I don't have to worry about it any more. I admit that I've often prayed hard about these things. Maybe you've done that too. You've cried and you've cried, and you prayed and you prayed, and you couldn't go to sleep at night. One time when I was doing that, God told me, "Hush, Thelma, I heard you the first time!" In this battle, I have to remember what I've told God— and that I've already given everything to him—the situation, the struggles, the issues that keep me awake at night.

Sometimes I say, "Okay, God, I give it all to you. I won't bother about it ever again. I won't worry. I'll be content." Then suddenly I'm whining, "But, God, you haven't done anything about this!" Can you relate? Our hopes get built up when we think we're trusting him, and we began to rejoice in what we think we see and then suddenly it seems like our faith and trust go down a very steep hill. Keep fighting and keep your faith strong! Fighting for your family is hard, but it's sure worth it.

And may I encourage you? If you're fighting for your family in whatever way, whatever the situation, remember that God knows what you're fighting, and he has the help and solution for you. In all these years that I've been fighting for my son, I've been clinging to God's promise that he will redeem the children of the righteous: "Be assured… the offspring of the righteous will be delivered" (Proverbs 11:21). One of these days that deliverance will be a reality.

And I believe there's finally some positive progress in my son's situation. "The race is not to the swift, nor the battle to the strong" (Ecclesiastes 9:11). There is victory for those who trust in the Lord and who hold out until the end.

Never give up on what you're praying for.

Never give up the fight.

Never, ever give up.

What Are Your Thoughts?

❅ But don't just take my word regarding persevering. As God encourages you via these passages in his Word, write down your heart's response to each one as a prayer to him or as an expression of your situation.

> But the one who endures to the end will be saved (Matthew 24:13).

> We rejoice in our sufferings, knowing that suffering produces endurance, and endurance produces character, and character produces hope (Romans 5:3-4).

> May you be strengthened with all power, according to his glorious might, for all endurance and patience with joy (Colossians 1:11).

> If we endure, we will also reign with him (2 Timothy 2:12).

> For you have need of endurance, so that when you have done the will of God you may receive what is promised (Hebrews 10:36).

Let us run with endurance the race that is set before us,
looking to Jesus, the founder and perfecter of our faith,
who for the joy that was set before him endured the cross,
despising the shame, and is seated at the right hand of the
throne of God. Consider him who endured from sinners
such hostility against himself, so that you may not grow
weary or fainthearted (Hebrews 12:1-3).

It is for discipline that you have to endure. God is treat-
ing you as sons (Hebrews 12:7).

Now, on the side, may I also add this? When it comes to dealing with struggling family members (and here's the grandmother and
great-grandmother coming out in me), don't enable. I had to learn
this. Enabling your loved ones in their negative behavior is never the
way to go. It doesn't help. Pray about your situation and ask God to
give you guidance.

Deborah the Fighter

When I think of someone who's a fighter, I like to think of Deborah
in the Old Testament. She was a judge and prophetess in Israel. Deborah "arose as a mother in Israel" (Judges 5:7). And she's shown to be
the most godly of all the leaders in the book of Judges. Deborah knew
about combat because she was a warrior herself—a mighty warrior.

The man in charge of some of Israel's fighting forces was named
Barak. Deborah summoned him and told him God's announcement
that it was time to take care of the enemies of God's people, especially the
Canaanite king who was tormenting them. "The people of Israel cried
out to the LORD for help," for this king "had 900 chariots of iron and
he oppressed the people of Israel cruelly for twenty years" (Judges 4:3).

Deborah passed along to Barak instructions from God: He was to recruit 10,000 men to go up against Sisera, the commander of the Canaanite army. God promised Barak victory: "I will draw out Sisera, the general of Jabin's army, to meet you by the river Kishon with his chariots and his troops, and I will give him into your hand" (Judges 4:7).

But Barak responded by saying he was staying put unless Deborah came along: "Barak said to her, 'If you will go with me, I will go, but if you will not go with me, I will not go'" (verse 8). Can't you just imagine Deborah rolling her eyes at that? Deborah agreed to go, but she told Barak that he would not get credit for the victory because of his unwillingness. Instead God would deliver Sisera into the hand of a woman.

"Then Deborah arose and went with Barak" (verse 9). She went with him into combat, along with the thousands of men who answered Barak's call to battle. Sisera quickly led his mighty Canaanite army to meet them, along with those 900 chariots of iron. As the enemy drew near, Deborah—with the heart and mind of a true military leader for God's people—turned to Barak and sounded the call to battle: "Up! For this is the day in which the LORD has given Sisera into your hand. Does not the LORD go out before you?" (Judges 4:14).

So the battle began—and God had a plan for it. He sent both earthquake and a torrent of rain to confuse the Canaanites and cause their chariots to sink into the mud. The victory was God's!

> And the LORD routed Sisera and all his chariots and all his army before Barak by the edge of the sword...And Barak pursued the chariots and the army to Harosheth-hagoyim, and all the army of Sisera fell by the edge of the sword; not a man was left (Judges 4:15-16).

Only General Sisera managed to escape. He slipped out of his useless chariot and fled on foot. He found his way to a friendly face—to the dwelling of a man the Canaanites were at peace with. This man's wife happened to be at home alone when Sisera straggled in. Jael went out to meet him. She invited him inside to eat, drink, and rest. She made him very comfortable and well-hidden.

But she had a plan.

While Sisera was sleeping, Jael crept up with a mallet and tent peg. She set that spike to his temple and drove it through his head and into the ground.

Jael received credit for finishing the victory that God had ordained and orchestrated that day. And everything happened just as Deborah had said it would.

What Are Your Thoughts?

❧ What impresses you most in this story about Deborah?

Isn't our God amazing, wonderful, and consistent? He provides solutions and follows through on his Word. He draws on his vast resources to accomplish his will. And he will fight *for* you—although you might not understand how he's going to reach the goal. Do you trust him enough to say, "Okay, God, I'm ready to work with you. I'm going to submit to you and follow your lead. Please help me win my battle."

Actually, the battle is not yours anyway. Whatever or whoever you're fighting, whether it's for your family, your business, your income, or your health, this battle *is not* yours. "The battle is the LORD's" (1 Samuel 17:47). That's what David said when he went out to meet Goliath. *The battle is the Lord's.* Ultimately that's true in every battle that's worth fighting. Young David, who as a shepherd boy had fought and killed lions and bears while defending the sheep he was guarding, knew firsthand the truth of this concept. And God wants you and me to grasp it just as thoroughly. He wants us to sing out that truth, just like the psalm writers did:

> For not in my bow do I trust,
> nor can my sword save me.
> But you have saved us from our foes...
> In God we have boasted continually,

and we will give thanks to your name forever
(Psalm 44:6-8).

The king is not saved by his great army;
a warrior is not delivered by his great strength.
The war horse is a false hope for salvation,
and by its great might it cannot rescue.
Behold, the eye of the LORD is on those who fear him,
on those who hope in his steadfast love,
that he may deliver their soul from death
and keep them alive in famine (Psalm 33:16-19).

What Are Your Thoughts?

❀ What are the big truths in those two quotes from the book of Psalms
that are *yours* to hold on to in faith?

God wants us to be as wise as Solomon in comprehending this truth:

No wisdom, no understanding, no counsel
can avail against the LORD.
The horse is made ready for the day of battle,
but the victory belongs to the LORD (Proverbs 21:30-31).

❀ What does it mean to you that the *victory belongs to the Lord?* Does
this change your approach or actions?

The Battle Is the Lord's

The Scriptures tell us of an incident, many years after David's time, when this truth that *the battle is the Lord's* became especially alive and powerful. Enemy nations were again threatening Israel. Jehoshaphat was Israel's king, and his scouts came and reported, "A great multitude is coming against you" (2 Chronicles 20:2). The king and people's response is a model for what you and I need to do in the spiritual warfare we fight.

Jehoshaphat didn't respond by being cocky and boastful. No, "Jehoshaphat was afraid" (20:3). But he dealt with his fear in the right way, and he led his people in the right direction: Jehoshaphat "set his face *to seek the* LORD, and proclaimed a fast throughout all Judah. And Judah assembled to *seek help from the* LORD; from all the cities of Judah they came to *seek the* LORD" (verses 3-4).

As they sought the Lord together, Jehoshaphat acknowledged their desperate condition, and their only hope: "O our God...we are powerless against this great horde that is coming against us. We do not know what to do, but *our eyes are on you*" (verse 12).

What Are Your Thoughts?

❈ In the struggles, issues, and obstacles you face today, what do you need to do to *seek the Lord* and focus your eyes on him? How will you get started?

While Jehoshaphat and the people were gathered before the Lord, God graciously gave them a word of truth and prophecy—an encouraging message that we need to hear again and again!

> And the Spirit of the LORD came upon Jahaziel...in the midst of the assembly. And he said, "Listen, all Judah and inhabitants of Jerusalem and King Jehoshaphat: Thus says the LORD to you, '*Do not be afraid* and *do not be dismayed* at this great horde, for *the battle is not yours but God's*. Tomorrow go down against them. Behold, they

will come up by the ascent of Ziz. You will find them at
the end of the valley, east of the wilderness of Jeruel. *You
will not need to fight in this battle. Stand firm, hold your
position, and see the salvation of the* LORD *on your behalf,
O Judah and Jerusalem.' Do not be afraid and do not be
dismayed.* Tomorrow go out against them, and *the* LORD
will be with you" (verses 14-17).

Can you imagine how encouraging that message from the Lord was
to the king and the people? Look at how they responded:

> Then Jehoshaphat bowed his head with his face to the
> ground, and all Judah and the inhabitants of Jerusalem
> fell down before the LORD, worshiping the LORD. And
> the Levites, of the Kohathites and the Korahites, stood
> up to praise the LORD, the God of Israel, with a very loud
> voice (verses 18-19).

When God prepares us for the battle that he will fight for us, we
get the awesome job and pleasure of praising and thanking and worshiping him!

What Are Your Thoughts?

❀ Pause for a moment now and praise and thank the Lord for who he
is and what he has done for you. Tell him how much you appreciate what he's going to do for you and how he will help you in the
struggles you face.

After King Jehoshaphat and the people praised God, they went out
the next day to do battle. The king reminded the Israelites of God's
support:

> And they rose early in the morning and went out into

the wilderness of Tekoa. And when they went out, Jehoshaphat stood and said, "Hear me, Judah and inhabitants of Jerusalem! Believe in the LORD your God, and you will be established; believe his prophets, and you will succeed" (verse 20).

Do you hear that? Did you note how healthy faith is linked strongly to the recognition that the battle is the Lord's? Jehoshaphat then made sure that the praise and worship would continue:

And when he had taken counsel with the people, he appointed those who were to sing to the LORD and praise him in holy attire, as they went before the army, and say, "Give thanks to the LORD, for his steadfast love endures forever" (verse 21).

Oh, can you imagine walking in that worshiping throng that day? Wouldn't it be thrilling to be marching forward into battle, confident and brave in the sure knowledge of God's love and support? Don't you want to experience that in your life? Don't you want to move forward so confidently in your life? I know I do. And the great news is that *we can!*

Forward to the Valley of Blessing

Let's see what happens next in the life of the Israelites.

And when they began to sing and praise, the LORD set an ambush against the men of Ammon, Moab, and Mount Seir, who had come against Judah, so that they were routed. For the men of Ammon and Moab rose against the inhabitants of Mount Seir, devoting them to destruction, and when they had made an end of the inhabitants of Seir, they all helped to destroy one another (2 Chronicles 20:22-23).

What surer picture could there be than to show his people the truth, the reality, that the *battle is the Lord's!*

> When Judah came to the watchtower of the wilderness, they looked toward the horde, and behold, there were dead bodies lying on the ground; none had escaped (verse 24)

After taking the plunder from their enemy's deserted camp (it took them three days!), the people came together again to worship God:

> On the fourth day they assembled in the Valley of Beracah, for there they blessed the LORD. Therefore the name of that place has been called the Valley of Beracah to this day (verse 26).

"Valley of Beracah" means "Valley of Blessing." And that's where the Lord wants to take us, which is exactly where we want to be, isn't it? And blessings bring so much joy:

> Then they returned, every man of Judah and Jerusalem, and Jehoshaphat at their head, returning to Jerusalem with joy, for the LORD had made them rejoice over their enemies. They came to Jerusalem with harps and lyres and trumpets, to the house of the LORD (verses 27-28).

God had given them victory. He had granted them success, and they didn't take this for granted. They didn't forget about it or just move on with life. No, they offered God fresh new praise and worship! And now their testimony to the nations was stronger than ever (Just like our own testimony for the Lord will be stronger than ever when we trust him to fight our battles). The effect was powerful:

> And the fear of God came on all the kingdoms of the countries when they heard that the LORD had fought against the enemies of Israel (verse 29).

And with the blessing, came peace:

> So the realm of Jehoshaphat was quiet, for his God gave him rest all around (2 Chronicles 20:30).

What a story! And it can be our story too—yours and mine!

14

For Spiritual Warfare

Yes, our battle is the Lord's. That's why, a few years ago, when I was more desperately sick than I have ever been and the doctors told me I was going to die, I could say, "Okay, God, take this and use it for your glory."

Yes, there are times during the battle when we get so pent up in fighting our war that we get bitter, angry, and vengeful. That's human. But when we fight against the wiles of the devil, which is the war we're in every day—and your heart has been bleeding and everything seems wrong—*trust in God.* He's going to bring you through. He really will. Just hang on! He may not solve the problems like we'd prefer, but he knows what we need and what is best.

Have there been situations where you felt that the more you trusted God, the worse things got? You asked, "Why do bad things happen to good people?" That's such a common question for us. Well, I know I don't have *all* the answers, but I found a good one in Romans 8:29. You're probably familiar with the verse before that: "And we know that for those who love God all things work together for good, for those who are called according to his purpose." But don't stop there! Let's go on to the next verse: "For those whom he foreknew he also predestined to be conformed to the image of his Son, in order that he might be the firstborn among many brothers." What does this mean? Everything that happens to us needs to be directly connected with the kingdom of God so we can become more like Jesus.

Deborah's Exemplary Qualities

Let's go back and think about Deborah, a judge and prophetess of Israel. She had some attributes that you and I are wise to emulate, especially as we consider the spiritual warfare we face.

Deborah was committed to fulfilling her calling. Did you know God has a calling on everybody's life? God has given everyone a purpose and a plan. Everyone has a ministry from him. If you know him, you want to actively participate in his plan for you! You may be called to send encouraging cards to make people feel better. You may pick up the telephone and say, "I was thinking of you today, and I want to encourage you." Your sweet touch is a representative of the touch of the Master's hand.

Do you know your calling? Do you know why God created you? I know I've asked you that before, but is the answer clear in your heart and mind?

What Are Your Thoughts?

🌼 Write down your mission and calling from the Lord as you understand it.

Deborah knew how to hear from God. She knew how to listen. God can talk to us any way he wants to. He can speak through the words on a billboard. He can tell us something through a song. He can talk to us through a friend (although he usually provides confirmation directly to us), or through a dream. He can communicate with us through whatever he wants to use. And our responsibility is to unstop our deaf ears so we can hear what he's saying. We need to take the shades off our eyes so we can see and get the shackles off our feet so we can dance.

What Are Your Thoughts?

🌼 Has God been trying to get *your* attention? If yes, how has he been doing that?

Deborah was unafraid to fight. We don't have to be afraid because God is with us and the battle is his. He's also told us how to fight and provided what we need. He's given us our battle instructions, and it's our responsibility to comprehend and follow his orders.

What Are Your Thoughts?

- Study these powerful verses from Ephesians 6:10-20. Respond to each verse by writing down what it teaches you about your battle-plan—your strategy, tactics, and weaponry for the spiritual warfare you're in.

> Finally, be strong in the Lord and in the strength of his might (Ephesians 6:10).

> Put on the whole armor of God, that you may be able to stand against the schemes of the devil (verse 11).

> For we do not wrestle against flesh and blood, but against the rulers, against the authorities, against the cosmic powers over this present darkness, against the spiritual forces of evil in the heavenly places (verse 12).

> Therefore take up the whole armor of God, that you may be able to withstand in the evil day, and having done all, to stand firm (verse 13).

Stand therefore, having fastened on the belt of truth...
(verse 14).

and having put on the breastplate of righteousness...
(verse 14).

and, as shoes for your feet, having put on the readiness
given by the gospel of peace (verse 15).

In all circumstances take up the shield of faith, with
which you can extinguish all the flaming darts of the
evil one...(verse 16).

and take the helmet of salvation, and the sword of the
Spirit, which is the word of God...(verse 17).

praying at all times in the Spirit, with all prayer and supplication. To that end keep alert with all perseverance,
making supplication for all the saints (verse 18).

The Power of Obedience

There's one more of Deborah's qualities we need to look at: *Deborah was obedient.* She gave Barak the message God told her to give him. God's Word says, "To obey is better than sacrifice" (1 Samuel 15:22). It really is!

If you're like me, a lot of times you don't feel like being obedient. Sometimes God may tell you to do something that to you seems foolish or ineffective, but I encourage you to move ahead and follow his instructions. I remember a time when I needed to quickly release $26,000 for a debt payment. I asked, as I usually do, "God, how do you want me to deal with this?" And God told me to give a certain person $2.60. And I thought, *Oh, that would be so awkward and embarrassing!* But God substantiated the fact that this is what he wanted me to do, so I did exactly as he said.

Then I sensed him telling me to send a certain ministry a gift of $26. That a was a bit easier to do than the $2.60 gift. I did that job too.

On the Saturday before the Monday that I needed the $26,000, I received a phone call from a real estate title company that was handling a transaction of mine. I had sold a house that I didn't know I wanted to sell until a lady asked, "Will you sell it?" And I answered, "Yes, I will."

So on that particular Saturday, the person from the title company called and said, "Mrs. Wells, I have a check here for you, but I'll be on vacation next week. Can you come in today and pick it up?"

I said, "Yes, ma'am." So I went down to their office and picked up the check, and it was for $33,000. God does exceedingly abundantly over and above what we ask or think or imagine!

When Monday came, I was able to fulfill my debt obligation. When I handed over the money, I asked the man, "Sir, do you believe in God?" He said, "Yes." And I said, "Let's have church then!" And I told him the story of what had happened and how the money had been released for me. There in this man's office we thanked God for his miracle-working power.

Obedience—whatever God tells you to do, do it.

What Are Your Thoughts?

🙣 Express in a new way your commitment to obey Jesus, your Lord and Master.

A Singing Faith

After Deborah and Barak were victorious, what do you think they did? They sang! They gave praise to God through song. And their song is preserved forever in Judges 5. And we can sing in our times of battle and victory too! We can rejoice over all that God has done and will do for us.

As you're fighting the battle, I encourage you to sing (or say) in your spirit these words from Psalm 100. They're the same words Jehoshaphat and the Israelites sang on their way to battle and to the Valley of Blessing: "The Lord is good; his steadfast love endures forever."

And there's so much more you can sing and praise him for as well. In fact, let me ask you: Have you ever tried giving a knockdown count to the devil? You've seen it in prize fighting—where the referee starts counting, and once he reaches ten the downed boxer has officially lost the bout. Let's you and me give a knockdown count to the devil. Ten words from the Lord will do it. You can say or sing these ten things in your spirit as you're fighting!

1. *The joy of the Lord is my strength.* Yes, that's exactly what God's Word tells us: "For the joy of the LORD is your strength" (Nehemiah 8:10).

What Are Your Thoughts?

🙣 Copy this verse and then note how it encourages you.

2. *Patience builds my character and character builds my hope.* "We rejoice in our sufferings, knowing that suffering produces endurance,

and endurance produces character, and character produces hope" (Romans 5:3-4).

🏵 Copy these verses and then note how they encourage you.

3. *I'll be anxious for nothing; instead I'll pray with thanksgiving.* "Do not be anxious about anything, but in everything by prayer and supplication with thanksgiving let your requests be made known to God" (Philippians 4:6).

🏵 Copy this verse and then note how it encourages you.

4. *God's perfect love casts out all my fear.* "There is no fear in love, but perfect love casts out fear" (1 John 4:18).

🏵 Copy this verse and then note how it encourages you.

5. *I'll be content, no matter what.* "I have learned in whatever situation I am to be content" (Philippians 4:11).

🏵 Copy this verse and then note how it encourages you.

6. *Hope does not disappoint when I hope in God.* "Now hope does not disappoint, because the love of God has been poured out in our hearts by the Holy Spirit who was given to us" (Romans 5:5 NKJV). "Hope in God; for I shall again praise him, my salvation and my God" (Psalm 42:11).

❧ Copy these verses and then note how they encourage you.

7. *I will have self-control because it is a fruit of the Spirit.* "The fruit of the Spirit is...self-control" (Galatians 5:22-23).

❧ Copy these verses and then note how they encourage you.

8. *I will have a sound mind, because that is God's gift to me.* "God has not given us a spirit of fear, but of power and of love and of a sound mind" (2 Timothy 1:7 NKJV).

❧ Copy this verse and then note how it encourages you.

9. *The Spirit of God helps me fight and encourages me.* I trust in God. It's "not by might, nor by power, but by my Spirit, says the LORD of hosts" (Zechariah 4:6). Yes, thank you, God, for your Spirit who moves in us, and works in us, and fights for us!

❧ Copy this verse and then note how it encourages you.

10. *I'm not ashamed of the gospel of Jesus Christ!* The gospel is the reason we can walk by faith. "I am not ashamed of the gospel, for it is the power of God for salvation to everyone who believes. For in it the righteousness of God is revealed *from faith for faith...*" (Romans 1:16). "Without faith it is impossible to please [God]" (Hebrews 11:6).

❊ Copy these verses and then note how they encourage you.

These ten reasons are why I boldly say, "God, I now can walk in faith because you've taught me that I can trust you, and love you, and hold your hand, and lean on your everlasting arms. You protect me and keep me."

Let's Pray

Thank you, God! Build us up and fortify us in our battle. Right here and now we willingly say, "We surrender all." We give you our marriages, our children, and our homes. We dedicate our jobs and finances to you. We surrender our health to you too. Yes, we surrender everything. Help us do this every day. And thank you for accepting us as we are and for loving us as your children. In Jesus' precious name. Amen.

15

Exercising Faith for Spiritual Victory

Yes, we're growing more bold and confident to say, "Lord, I'm ready to walk by faith!" We so desperately need that boldness and confidence because we are in a battle where the enemy wants to do everything possible to disturb, discourage, and defeat us. So we need to keep our faith toned up and strong.

Before we enter Part 5, the final section of this book, let's focus on reinforcing our faith for spiritual victory. I know it's easy to read the truths in the Word of God and based on the Word of God and think, *Yeah, that's good stuff.* But when the truths of God's Word confront and convict us and we understand they're causing us to grow stronger and mature spiritually, we are better able to receive them as loving gifts from our heavenly Father.

The Lord gives us a call to battle in 1 Peter 5:8-9—a passage that identifies our enemy, his strategy, and drills us in the proper response:

> Be sober-minded; be watchful. Your adversary the devil prowls around like a roaring lion, seeking someone to devour. Resist him, *firm in your faith,* knowing that the same kinds of suffering are being experienced by your brotherhood throughout the world.

What Are Your Thoughts?

❀ If you are *not* firm in your faith, what do you think is likely to be the outcome when you're attacked by the prowling enemy—the devil?

❀ In your own words, describe what it means to be "firm in your faith"? What does this look like in your life?

Our Best Example of Faith

Jesus is "the founder and perfecter of our faith" (Hebrews 12:2). In the realm of spiritual warfare, he demonstrated great faith for us in his encounter with Satan and his tricks in the wilderness. Here is Luke's version of that encounter:

> And Jesus, full of the Holy Spirit, returned from the Jordan and was led by the Spirit in the wilderness for forty days, being tempted by the devil. And he ate nothing during those days. And when they were ended, he was hungry.
>
> The devil said to him, "If you are the Son of God, command this stone to become bread."
>
> And Jesus answered him, "It is written, 'Man shall not live by bread alone.'"
>
> And the devil took him up and showed him all the kingdoms of the world in a moment of time, and said to him, "To you I will give all this authority and their glory, for it has been delivered to me, and I give it to whom I will. If you, then, will worship me, it will all be yours."
>
> And Jesus answered him, "It is written, 'You shall worship the Lord your God, and him only shall you serve.'"

And he took him to Jerusalem and set him on the pinnacle of the temple and said to him, "If you are the Son of God, throw yourself down from here, for it is written, 'He will command his angels concerning you, to guard you,' and 'On their hands they will bear you up, lest you strike your foot against a stone.'"

And Jesus answered him, "It is said, 'You shall not put the Lord your God to the test.'"

And when the devil had ended every temptation, he departed from him until an opportune time.

And Jesus returned in the power of the Spirit to Galilee.

What Are Your Thoughts?

❀ What are the most important ways you see Jesus demonstrating his trust in his Father in this Luke passage?

❀ How does this passage demonstrate the *power* of faith in the midst of spiritual warfare?

❀ What are the most important ways from this Luke passage that Jesus serves as an example of faith for us in our spiritual warfare encounters?

Faith's Armor

In Ephesians 4, Paul says that all of us believers in Christ share in "one *faith*" (verse 5). He mentions the variety of spiritual giftedness among the body of Christ so that we can "all attain to the unity of the faith" (verse 13). Then he goes on to spiritual warfare by telling us to "give no opportunity to the devil" (verse 27).

What Are Your Thoughts?

❧ In what ways might we open up opportunities to the devil in our lives? What kinds of opportunities is the devil looking for?

At the end of his letter to the Ephesians, Paul turns more fully to the topic of spiritual warfare. In Ephesians 6:10-20, he describes the battle we face as well as our spiritual armor for that battle. He mentions specifically "the shield of faith," but looking closely, we see that all aspects of our armor are tied to faith. First, notice the nature of the battle we face:

> Finally, be strong in the Lord and in the strength of his might. Put on the whole armor of God, that you may be able to stand against the schemes of the devil. For we do not wrestle against flesh and blood, but against the rulers, against the authorities, against the cosmic powers over this present darkness, against the spiritual forces of evil in the heavenly places (Ephesians 6:10-12).

What Are Your Thoughts?

❧ Based on the information given in those verses, why do you think spiritual warfare requires *faith*? What is the *truth* in that passage that you must understand and believe to be effective in spiritual warfare?

Paul continued,

> Therefore take up the whole armor of God, that you may be able to withstand in the evil day, and having done all, to stand firm. Stand therefore, having fastened on the belt of truth, and having put on the breastplate of righteousness, and, as shoes for your feet, having put on the readiness given by the gospel of peace. In all circumstances take up *the shield of faith,* with which you can extinguish all the flaming darts of the evil one; and take the helmet of salvation, and the sword of the Spirit, which is the word of God, praying at all times in the Spirit, with all prayer and supplication (Ephesians 6:13-18).

What Are Your Thoughts?

🎖 In what ways do you see faith connected with all these pieces of armor?

The apostle James reminds us that "God opposes the proud, but gives grace to the humble" (James 4:6). Then he tells us, "Submit yourselves therefore to God. Resist the devil, and he will flee from you" (verse 7).

What Are Your Thoughts?

🎖 How is *faith* connected to the kind of *humility* James speaks of?

❀ How is pride connected with unbelief?

🎗 How is faith linked with submitting yourself to God, as James says to do?

🎗 In what ways does it take faith to "resist the devil"?

In the midst of the spiritual warfare Peter was undergoing, notice what Jesus did on his behalf:

> Simon, Simon, behold, Satan demanded to have you, that he might sift you like wheat, but I have prayed for you that your faith may not fail. And when you have turned again, strengthen your brothers (Luke 22:31-32).

What Are Your Thoughts?

🎗 Why did Jesus pray that Peter's "faith may not fail"? What is the significance of this?

🎗 Did Peter's faith "fail" when he later denied Jesus three times (Luke 22:54-62)?

🎗 When did Peter "turn again" (Luke 22:32)?

❧ In what way was faith required for this turnaround on Peter's part?

❧ In what ways was faith required on Peter's part to strengthen his brothers?

If we will remember these truths about Jesus, we'll be encouraged and strengthened during our battles:

> He is able to save to the uttermost those who draw near to God through him, since he always lives *to make intercession for them* (Hebrews 7:25).

> For Christ has entered...into heaven itself, now to *appear in the presence of God on our behalf* (Hebrews 9:24).

> He poured out his soul to death and was numbered with the transgressors; yet he bore the sin of many, and *makes intercession for the transgressors* (Isaiah 53:12).

> Christ Jesus is the one who died—more than that, who was raised—who is at the right hand of God, who indeed is *interceding for us* (Romans 8:34).

What Are Your Thoughts?

❧ In Jesus' intercession for *you* before God, do you think he is praying "that your faith may not fail"—just as he prayed for Simon Peter?

❀ If you *do* believe Christ is praying this for you, what do you believe will determine the answer?

The Promise of Victory

Near the very end of his letter to the Romans, Paul writes:

The God of peace will soon crush Satan under your feet. The grace of our Lord Jesus Christ be with you (Romans 16:20).

What Are Your Thoughts?

❀ What is the promise in that verse that you can claim by faith?

❀ What will this mean, in a practical way, for you?

Listen to these words from John:

Everyone who has been born of God overcomes the world. And this is the victory that has overcome the world—*our faith*. Who is it that overcomes the world except the one who *believes* that Jesus is the Son of God? (1 John 5:4-5).

What Are Your Thoughts?

✿ According to that truth, you can be assured of spiritual victory. Acknowledge and respond to that truth now in a grateful, written prayer to God.

PART 6

Faith That Sings

16

Legacy

I've told you about my great-grandmother and the influence she had on me. What a legacy she has left me! And what an example for me to follow. She taught me how to love people, how to nurture people, and how to feed people. We had good food to serve folks all the time.

My great-grandmother also taught me the truth of Titus 2:3-4, which says that the older women should teach the younger women how to do the right thing (that's the Thelma Wells paraphrase). I know you understand why I was so close to my great-grandmother, but eventually that meant I had to come to grips with some faith issues.

Letting Go

Granny eventually got sick, had several strokes, and was bedridden. Her doctor said to me, "You're going to have to put her somewhere because you can't take care of her."

And I answered, "I'm not putting her anywhere. When she was already in her old age, and I was only two years old and couldn't take care of myself, she took me in and cared for me. I will not put her anywhere; I'm going to take care of her myself."

And so I did. And as I'm sure you know or can imagine, there's a lot to caring for someone who's bedridden. Because of the stroke she couldn't swallow well. So I often got an eyedropper, filled it with water, squirted it in her mouth, and then massaged her neck so she could get moisture into her throat.

Oh, I loved that woman! And I still love her today. When the time came for her to go home to the Lord, I didn't like it. I didn't like it at all. I knew she was an invalid and could do nothing for herself, and she'd always said, "Baby, when I can't do anything for myself and I'm not useful to anybody, I want God to take me home." That was her desire—but it wasn't mine.

My husband and other people kept saying to me, "You've got to let her go, Thelma."

And I would answer, "Hush, I'm not letting her go. I'm going to keep her with me." And I prayed, "God, when you get ready to take my granny, don't take her before you take me. Take me first. I don't think I can live without her."

One day after caring for her, I went out and sat on the front porch. I looked up to the sky and said, "God, I don't want to release her. I don't want her to go. I want you to heal her. I want her to get back up and be to me what she was. But it's okay, God, if it's your will, to take her if she's ready to go home." And I prayed, "Help me, God, 'cause I can't do this without you." After I prayed that, I felt a special peace, a peace that I don't understand and can't really describe. I said, "Okay, God, if you're ready to take her, help me."

That was on a Thursday. I kept feeling that peace as I went through Friday and Saturday. Then came Sunday. Granny always loved Sundays. And that Sunday was the most powerful, wonderful, gorgeous day ever for my great-grandmother. The sun was brighter that Sunday, the grass was greener, and the worship was more powerful.

My mother and my sister and my grandfather and other family members were there at our house, and we were sitting in the living room. I heard my granny sigh. And she was gone.

And I had faith enough in God to believe and to know that he had prepared me for that moment, for I had relinquished my desire to his will. Granny was gone, but I knew exactly where she was. She went home to be with the Lord. Some people say when a loved one dies, "I lost my mother" or "I lost my grandfather." But I didn't lose Granny!

I know exactly where she is. And I know that one glad morning when my life is over, I'm going to go there too. I believe she's in that great cloud of witnesses looking down on us today. Yes, I believe that with all my heart—that those who die in the Lord go from life to life. And I love that!

Cloud of Witnesses

That phrase "cloud of witnesses" is from the opening of Hebrews 12, and it's referring to all the people just talked about in Hebrews 11. That passage—the great eleventh chapter in Hebrews—is known as the "Hall of Faith." I believe my granny is there waiting for me (and for all of us) to come and join her. Let's make our way through that Hall of Faith and see what we can discover.

17

Our Own Hall of Faith

I love the Hall of Faith passage in Hebrews 11. I'm sure you've read it. And if you haven't, it's a wonderful place to go to discover what was accomplished by the people of great faith mentioned in the Bible. So many of them are mentioned by name and discussed in detail. It's so encouraging! To get the most from this section of God's Word, let's go through it together.

Faith Is...

Now faith is the assurance of things hoped for, the conviction of things not seen. For by it the people of old received their commendation. By faith we understand that the universe was created by the word of God, so that what is seen was not made out of things that are visible (Hebrews 11:1-3).

What Are Your Thoughts?

❦ What do these verses teach you about the meaning and definition and example of faith?

By Faith, Abel…

Remember Cain and Abel?

> By faith Abel offered to God a more acceptable sacrifice
> than Cain, through which he was commended as righ-
> teous, God commending him by accepting his gifts. And
> through his faith, though he died, he still speaks (verse 4).

What Are Your Thoughts?

❀ What encouragement does this verse give you about your faith?

By Faith, Enoch…

Enoch walked in faith. The book of Genesis emphasizes this by telling us *twice* that "Enoch walked with God" (5:22 and 24). Hebrews
11:5 tells us:

> By faith Enoch was taken up so that *he should not see*
> *death,* and he was not found, because God had taken
> him. Now before he was taken he was commended as
> having pleased God (Hebrews 11:5).

And that leads to a wonderful observation about faith:

> And without faith it is impossible to please [God], for
> whoever would draw near to God must believe that he
> exists and that he rewards those who seek him (verse 6).

What Are Your Thoughts?

❀ What encouragement do these two verses give you about your faith?

❀ What is your personal expectation of being *rewarded* as you seek the Lord?

By Faith, Noah...

What a powerful example of faith we have in Noah!

> By faith Noah, being warned by God concerning events as yet unseen, in reverent fear constructed an ark for the saving of his household. By this he condemned the world and became an heir of the righteousness that comes by faith (verse 7).

What Are Your Thoughts?

❀ What encouragement does this verse give you about your faith?

I've got to say this about Noah, can you imagine somebody telling you to build a boat when it had never even rained, let alone flooded? But Noah spent more than 120 years building what God told him to. I've often wondered what Mrs. Noah said. She must have thought, *You know, my husband is crazy. People are talking about him, and I don't like them talking about him, but he's lost his mind.*

Noah was out there building what? A *boat!* What for? *Rain.* What is "rain"?

But Noah had enough faith in God that he followed God's instructions exactly. This verse about Noah in Hebrews 11 confirms that "righteousness...comes by *faith.*" So of course we want to walk in faith! Faith in every way leads us into righteousness in Christ. That's worth exploring!

What Are Your Thoughts?

❀ What do the following passages tell you about faith leading to righteousness?

> To all those in Rome who are loved by God and called to be saints: Grace to you and peace from God our Father and the Lord Jesus Christ (Romans 1:7).

> But now the righteousness of God has been manifested apart from the law, although the Law and the Prophets bear witness to it—the righteousness of God through faith in Jesus Christ for all who believe (Romans 3:21-22).

> Gentiles who did not pursue righteousness have attained it, that is, a righteousness that is by faith; but...Israel who pursued a law that would lead to righteousness did not succeed in reaching that law. Why? Because they did not pursue it by faith, but as if it were based on works. They have stumbled over the stumbling stone (Romans 9:30-32).

> They have a zeal for God, but not according to knowledge. For, being ignorant of the righteousness that comes from God, and seeking to establish their own, they did not submit to God's righteousness. For Christ is the end of the law for righteousness to everyone who believes (Romans 10:2-4).

For through the Spirit, by faith, we ourselves eagerly wait
for the hope of righteousness (Galatians 5:5).

Indeed, I count everything as loss because of the surpassing worth of knowing Christ Jesus my Lord. For
his sake I have suffered the loss of all things and count
them as rubbish, in order that I may gain Christ and be
found in him, not having a righteousness of my own that
comes from the law, but that which comes through faith
in Christ, the righteousness from God that depends on
faith (Philippians 3:8-9).

By Faith, Abraham...

Abraham, faithful Abraham, comes next in the Hall of Faith. His
life is living testimony that righteousness comes by faith:

By faith Abraham obeyed when he was called to go out
to a place that he was to receive as an inheritance. And
he went out, not knowing where he was going. By faith
he went to live in the land of promise, as in a foreign
land, living in tents with Isaac and Jacob, heirs with him
of the same promise. For he was looking forward to the
city that has foundations, whose designer and builder is
God (Hebrews 11:8-10).

You know what Abraham did? He walked away from everything
that was his, and he left it all and went out not even knowing where he
would end up. Why? Because he was looking forward to something.

What Are Your Thoughts?

✿ Look again at this passage about Abraham. What was he looking forward to?

✿ What do you think that means?

✿ And what does it mean in relation to what *you* are looking forward to eternally?

By Faith, Sarah...

Next in the Hall of Faith comes Abraham's wife, Sarah. My great-grandmother's name was Sarah, and my sister's name is Sarah. So when I see the name *Sarah* in the Bible, I always smile. Do you know what happened to the biblical Sarah?

> By faith Sarah herself received power to conceive, even when she was past the age, since she considered him faithful who had promised (Hebrews 11:11).

Sarah knew God was faithful, but you know, that wasn't easy for her. One day Abraham was talking to a man of God (he was really God or an angel of God). This man told Abraham that Sarah was going to have a baby (Genesis 18). Sarah was eavesdropping. (That's something we women do well.) And when she heard him say she was going to have a baby, she laughed.

Now, it's not that Sarah didn't want a child, and it's not that she doubted God could give her a child in her old age. But she laughed at the very idea of an old woman such as herself getting pregnant.

Then the man of God asked, "Why did Sarah laugh?" And Sarah lied and said, "I did not laugh," because she was suddenly afraid (Genesis 18:14-15.)

But even though Sarah prevaricated, even though her faith wasn't perfect, even though her faith needed to mature and grow, she's listed in this Hall of Faith! Now that gives hope for you and me, doesn't it?

Seeking a Heavenly Home

Then Hebrews 11 turns back to Abraham. Abraham couldn't have received the blessing he did if it weren't for his wife, Sarah, and her faith.

> Therefore from one man, and him as good as dead, were born descendants as many as the stars of heaven and as many as the innumerable grains of sand by the seashore (Hebrews 11:12).

Here was a promise fulfilled—a promise that God had made more than once to Abraham:

> I will surely bless you, and I will surely multiply your offspring as the stars of heaven and as the sand that is on the seashore (Genesis 22:17).

That promise wasn't fulfilled in Abraham's time, but the apostle Paul dwells at length on Abraham's situation:

> For the promise to Abraham and his offspring that he would be heir of the world did not come through the law but through the righteousness of faith...That is why it depends on faith, in order that the promise may rest on grace and be guaranteed to all his offspring—not only to the adherent of the law but also to the one who shares the faith of Abraham, who is the father of us all, as it is

written, "I have made you the father of many nations"—
in the presence of the God in whom he believed, who
gives life to the dead and calls into existence the things
that do not exist (Romans 4:13,16-17).

There's a lot of information in that passage!

What Are Your Thoughts?

✿ What's the essence of this passage's message about God?

✿ And what's the essence of what this passage is telling us about
faith?

Let's hear more about Abraham's response to God's plan:

In hope he believed against hope, that he should become
the father of many nations, as he had been told, "So shall
your offspring be." He did not weaken in faith when he
considered his own body, which was as good as dead
(since he was about a hundred years old), or when he
considered the barrenness of Sarah's womb. No distrust
made him waver concerning the promise of God, but
he grew strong in his faith as he gave glory to God, fully
convinced that God was able to do what he had promised. That is why his faith was "counted to him as righteousness" (Romans 4:18-22).

What Are Your Thoughts?

✿ How exactly did Abraham's faith grow and deepen?

❀ How is this an example in your faith development and maturity?

The wonderful thing about this is how fully we are meant to share in Abraham's experience—and all because of Jesus!

> But the words "it was counted to him" were not written for [Abraham's] sake alone, but for ours also. It will be counted to us who believe in him who raised from the dead Jesus our Lord, who was delivered up for our trespasses and raised for our justification (Romans 4:23-25).

What Are Your Thoughts?

✿ What does that passage teach about the real *substance* of faith?

Oh what riches these are that we experience in Christ! Abraham saw those riches from a distance, but he hadn't yet experienced them. And that leads us to the next section of Hebrews 11.

Seeking a Heavenly Home

You see, that was true for all of those folks mentioned in Hebrews 11. They wouldn't see or experience the entire fulfillment of the promises God had given them. Not in their lifetimes. They had to go to their graves without experiencing the total reality of what God had given them glimpses of.

> These all died in faith, not having received the things
> promised, but having seen them and greeted them from
> afar, and having acknowledged that they were strangers
> and exiles on the earth (Hebrews 11:13).

Even though they didn't fully experience the accomplishments of God's promises, that didn't mean they weren't absolutely thrilled about them. No, with their spiritual vision they could *see* those promises fulfilled so they "greeted them from afar" with joy! They could do this because they knew this earth was not their true and ultimate home.

What Are Your Thoughts?

🌲 The people mentioned in the Hall of Faith were "strangers and exiles" in this world. Do you know what that means? And how that applies to you?

> For people who speak thus make it clear that they are
> seeking a homeland. If they had been thinking of that
> land from which they had gone out, they would have
> had opportunity to return. But as it is, they desire a bet-
> ter country, that is, a heavenly one. Therefore God is not
> ashamed to be called their God, for he has prepared for
> them a city (Hebrews 11:14-16).

What Are Your Thoughts?

🌲 According to this passage, what were these people really after?

✽ And because of their heart's true desire, how did God respond?

✽ What are you ultimately seeking in the deepest part of your soul?

By Faith, Abraham...

There's even more to see and marvel at in the faith Abraham had.

> By faith Abraham, when he was tested, offered up Isaac, and he who had received the promises was in the act of offering up his only son, of whom it was said, "Through Isaac shall your offspring be named." He considered that God was able even to raise him from the dead, from which, figuratively speaking, he did receive him back (Hebrews 11:17-19).

Can a father possibly experience a trial that's deeper and more profound than the testing God put Abraham through on Mount Moriah with his son Isaac? God told him, "Take your son, your only son Isaac, whom you love, and go to the land of Moriah, and offer him there as a burnt offering on one of the mountains of which I shall tell you" (Genesis 22:2). By *faith*, Abraham obeyed his loving Lord, even in such a troubling command. And that faith, that obedience, required concrete *actions*:

> So Abraham *rose* early in the morning, *saddled* his donkey, and *took* two of his young men with him, and his son Isaac. And he *cut* the wood for the burnt offering and *arose* and *went* to the place of which God had told him...
>
> And Abraham *took* the wood of the burnt offering and

laid it on Isaac his son. And he *took* in his hand the fire and the knife. So they went both of them together...

When they came to the place of which God had told him, Abraham *built* the altar there and *laid* the wood in order and *bound* Isaac his son and *laid* him on the altar, on top of the wood. Then Abraham *reached* out his hand and *took* the knife to slaughter his son (Genesis 22:3-10).

What Are Your Thoughts?

⚜ What specific steps of action is God asking you to take as you move forward in faith and obedience to him?

God, in his mercy and grace, rewarded Abraham's faith in a spectacular way:

> But the angel of the LORD called to him from heaven and said, "Abraham, Abraham!"
>
> And he said, "Here am I."
>
> He said, "Do not lay your hand on the boy or do anything to him, for now I know that you fear God, seeing you have not withheld your son, your only son, from me."
>
> And Abraham lifted up his eyes and looked, and behold, behind him was a ram, caught in a thicket by his horns. And Abraham went and took the ram and offered it up as a burnt offering instead of his son.
>
> So Abraham called the name of that place, "The LORD will provide"; as it is said to this day, "On the mount of the LORD it shall be provided."

What Are Your Thoughts?

✿ "The LORD will provide"—what a statement of faith, a motto of faith! What are you trusting in faith for God to provide in your situation?

In mercy and grace, God gave Abraham a profound reassurance of the promises he'd made:

> And the angel of the LORD called to Abraham a second time from heaven and said, "By myself I have sworn, declares the LORD, because you have done this and have not withheld your son, your only son, I will surely bless you, and I will surely multiply your offspring as the stars of heaven and as the sand that is on the seashore. And your offspring shall possess the gate of his enemies, and in your offspring shall all the nations of the earth be blessed, because you have obeyed my voice" (Genesis 22:15-18).

What Are Your Thoughts?

✿ This blessing for "all the nations of the earth"—how are you sharing in it right now?

❀ Why not praise and thank God right now for your share in this blessing?

By Faith, Isaac...Jacob...Joseph...

In the Hall of Faith, Abraham's faithful heritage continues with his son, grandson, and great-grandson.

> By faith Isaac invoked future blessings on Jacob and Esau. By faith Jacob, when dying, blessed each of the sons of Joseph, bowing in worship over the head of his staff. By faith Joseph, at the end of his life, made mention of the exodus of the Israelites and gave directions concerning his bones (Hebrews 11:20-22).

Let's look closer at the specific situations of these three men this passage commends. First, Isaac's blessing of Jacob:

> May God give you of the dew of heaven and of the fatness of the earth and plenty of grain and wine. Let peoples serve you, and nations bow down to you. Be lord over your brothers, and may your mother's sons bow down to you. Cursed be everyone who curses you, and blessed be everyone who blesses you! (Genesis 27:28-30).

What Are Your Thoughts?

✿ How did this blessing show Isaac's faith?

And then we have Isaac's blessing of his other son Esau:

> Behold, away from the fatness of the earth shall your dwelling be, and away from the dew of heaven on high. By your sword you shall live, and you shall serve your brother; but when you grow restless you shall break his yoke from your neck (Genesis 27:39-40).

What Are Your Thoughts?

🕸 If you know the full story (you may want to read Genesis 27), how does Isaac's blessing of Esau demonstrate Isaac's faith?

Next comes Jacob's blessing of Joseph's sons, Ephraim and Manasseh:

> The God before whom my fathers Abraham and Isaac walked, the God who has been my shepherd all my life long to this day, the angel who has redeemed me from all evil, bless the boys; and in them let my name be carried on, and the name of my fathers Abraham and Isaac; and let them grow into a multitude in the midst of the earth (Genesis 48:15-16).

What Are Your Thoughts?

🕸 How did this blessing demonstrate Jacob's faith?

And then we have Joseph's situation:

> And Joseph said to his brothers, "I am about to die, but God will visit you and bring you up out of this land to the land that he swore to Abraham, to Isaac, and to Jacob." Then Joseph made the sons of Israel swear, saying, "God will surely visit you, and you shall carry up my bones from here" (Genesis 50:24-25).

What Are Your Thoughts?

How did this incident demonstrate Joseph's faith?

By Faith, Moses...

Next in the Hall of Faith, we come to the faith of Moses.

> By faith Moses, when he was born, was hidden for three months by his parents, because they saw that the child was beautiful, and they were not afraid of the king's edict (Hebrews 11:23).

The faith being highlighted here is that of Moses' parents. And as we noted earlier, Moses grew into a man of great faith as well. His parents trained him up in the way he should go even though their time with him was so short.

In an earlier chapter we looked at this testimony from Hebrews 11 about the faith of Moses. Let's enjoy it again:

> By faith Moses, when he was grown up, refused to be called the son of Pharaoh's daughter, choosing rather to be mistreated with the people of God than to enjoy the fleeting pleasures of sin. He considered the reproach of Christ greater wealth than the treasures of Egypt, for he was looking to the reward (verses 24-26).

And there's more:

> By faith he left Egypt, not being afraid of the anger of the king, for he endured as seeing him who is invisible. By faith he kept the Passover and sprinkled the blood, so that the Destroyer of the firstborn might not touch them (verses 27-28).

Because of his faith, Moses became a fearless leader and a man of obedience to God.

By Faith, the People...

The faithful leadership of Moses allowed the people of Israel to demonstrate their faith as well: "By faith the people crossed the Red Sea as on dry land, but the Egyptians, when they attempted to do the same, were drowned" (verse 29).

A generation later, under the leadership of faithful Joshua, came another demonstration of the mighty power of faith: "By faith the walls of Jericho fell down after they had been encircled for seven days" (verse 30).

What Are Your Thoughts?

😵 Are there any "walls" you're facing that need to be brought down by faith? If so, talk to the Lord about it through writing while the faith of God's people at Jericho is fresh in your mind and heart.

By Faith, Rahab...

And the Hall of Faith list includes Rahab, a woman of Jericho: "By faith Rahab the prostitute did not perish with those who were disobedient, because she had given a friendly welcome to the spies" (verse 31). She was not an Israelite, but she knew enough about the God of Israel to worship and trust him. When Joshua sent spies into Jericho, she kept them safe from the enemy by hiding them. Listen as she explained her actions:

> I know that the LORD has given you the land, and that the fear of you has fallen upon us, and that all the inhabitants of the land melt away before you. For we have heard how the LORD dried up the water of the Red Sea before

you when you came out of Egypt, and what you did to
the two kings of the Amorites who were beyond the Jor-
dan, to Sihon and Og, whom you devoted to destruction. And as soon as we heard it, our hearts melted, and
there was no spirit left in any man because of you, for
the LORD your God, he is God in the heavens above and
on the earth beneath. Now then, please swear to me by
the LORD that, as I have dealt kindly with you, you also
will deal kindly with my father's house, and give me a
sure sign that you will save alive my father and mother,
my brothers and sisters, and all who belong to them, and
deliver our lives from death (Joshua 2:9-13).

What Are Your Thoughts?

❦ How do Rahab's words and actions demonstrate her sincere faith?

❦ What about Rahab's faith is an example for your own faith?

More Faith Heroes

There's so very much to learn about faith in Hebrews 11!

And what more shall I say? For time would fail me to
tell of Gideon, Barak, Samson, Jephthah, of David and
Samuel and the prophets—who through faith conquered kingdoms, enforced justice, obtained promises,
stopped the mouths of lions, quenched the power of fire,
escaped the edge of the sword, were made strong out of
weakness, became mighty in war, put foreign armies to

flight. Women received back their dead by resurrection. Some were tortured, refusing to accept release, so that they might rise again to a better life. Others suffered mocking and flogging, and even chains and imprisonment. They were stoned, they were sawn in two, they were killed with the sword. They went about in skins of sheep and goats, destitute, afflicted, mistreated—of whom the world was not worthy—wandering about in deserts and mountains, and in dens and caves of the earth (verses 32-38).

What Are Your Thoughts?

❀ What impression do you get from these verses regarding what faith is really all about?

And now the Hall of Faith circles back to you and me!

And all these, though commended through their faith, did not receive what was promised, since God had provided something better for us, that apart from us they should not be made perfect (verses 39-40).

What Are Your Thoughts?

❀ What is the "something better" for you and me that this passage refers to?

❀ What does that have to do with your faith?

The Perfecter of Our Faith

The encouragement and line of reasoning continues from Hebrews 11 directly into some glorious truths in Hebrews 12. Here's the climax, and it just bowls me over every time I read it!

> Therefore, since we are surrounded by so great a cloud of witnesses, let us also lay aside every weight, and sin which clings so closely, and let us run with endurance the race that is set before us, looking to Jesus, the founder and perfecter of our faith, who for the joy that was set before him endured the cross, despising the shame, and is seated at the right hand of the throne of God (Hebrews 12:1-2).

All those witnesses—"so great a cloud"! And "I want to be in that number when the saints go marching in," looking to Jesus and sharing in his joy. I hope right now, without a shadow of a doubt, that *you* will be in that number too. God has given you everything you need to say, "God, I'm ready to walk in faith." And now say it with assurance! "God, I'm *so* ready to walk in faith!"

And if you're not ready…now is a good time to get ready. And how do you go about doing that? It's not by doing. Doing good things will not save you. There are a lot of wonderful people in this world—nice people, lovely people, caring people, benevolent people, thoughtful people—who have one critical person missing from their lives: Jesus Christ. And he alone is "the founder and perfecter" of faith and he alone is the Savior and Lord who can take away our sins and draw us close to God.

The only way to get ready is to choose Jesus Christ. Believe in his love, his death, his resurrection, his overcoming death, his atonement for your sin, his interceding so that your relationship with God is restored. You only have to ask Jesus into your heart, saying, "Lord, I believe in you, I believe that you died and rose again on my behalf. I willingly choose you to be my Lord and Savior."

And then will you take this message to all the good people in the world who don't know Christ so they too can be part of that heavenly "cloud of witnesses"?

Confronting a Pagan Priest

While in Africa I decided one day to go to the shrine of a certain fetish priest. It was where he sacrificed animals. As I started out, people said, "You can't do that! You can't go there. The priest will kill you!" But as I walked along, I was whispering, "The blood of Jesus, the blood of Jesus, the blood of Jesus..." You know, don't you, that Jesus said, "Behold, I have given you authority to tread on serpents and scorpions, and over all the power of the enemy, and nothing shall hurt you" (Luke 10:19). So I walked up there to the shrine of that fetish priest. I thanked him for allowing us to come to his village, and then I asked him a question. I said, "Priest, what do you want most in your life?"

And he replied, "Peace."

And I said, "Oh, priest! I'm so glad you said that! Because everybody wants peace, and I can tell you how you can get it. I can tell you how to get peace so that you'll never have to sacrifice another animal." I went on. "You know, there was a man once who was killed by being stretched out and nailed to a rugged wooden cross. It was a humiliating death. And first they made fun of him by putting a crown of thorns on his head. The blood from his wounded head flowed down, and that blood flowing down was to give peace to *you*, priest."

And I said, "They then stretched his arms wide and put spikes in his hands to fasten him to that cross. But the blood that flowed from his pierced hands was flowing there for *you*, priest."

I said, "Oh, priest, they also put spikes in his feet, so he couldn't even move. And the blood from his wounded feet came down, and it came down to give *you* peace. And this peace is an everlasting peace. It will never change or wane. This peace will uphold you when times are hard, and this peace will help you do the right thing.

"Priest, you don't ever have to burn an animal again! For the man, Jesus Christ, has come to give you peace eternally." I told him how to receive Christ, and said, "Priest, will you repeat this special prayer after me?" And he did! He said a prayer of salvation.

And I'm going to give you an opportunity like that right now too. This is really a prayer of relinquishment and a prayer of invitation. It's a prayer to get everything you need from Jesus Christ, the Son of the living God, the anointed one, the Messiah, for indeed the anointing destroys the yoke of slavery. Will you pray this with me?

> *Dear Jesus, thank you for loving me. I know I'm not worthy. I know I've sinned. But you say to come as I am, so here I am. I'm wretched, undone, and somewhat confused because I'm not sure you can do what everybody says you can do. But by faith, Jesus, I ask you to come into my life—to live in me, and to forgive my sins, and to start cleaning me up as I grow in you so I can live more fully for you. Please do that. I'm trusting you. In your precious name I pray. Amen.*

If you've prayed that prayer, then you can say confidently,

"God, I'm ready to walk in faith!"

18

Exercising Faith for
Joyful Praise

Now comes the joy! Let's work together to build ourselves up in holy faith (Jude 20). Let's uncover how to exercise our faith through joyful praise to the Lord. When we think about the way faith leads to joyful praise, we are entering a realm beyond words. Our attempts to describe it fall short every time. Peter tells us, "Though you have not seen him, you love him. Though you do not now see him, you *believe in him* and rejoice with joy that is *inexpressible* and filled with glory" (1 Peter 1:8).

Faith in Jesus brings a joy that is inexpressible. But still we just can't stop trying to express it! And many of the writers in Scripture have done that as well. Reflect deeply on the verses highlighted in this chapter because all of them are full of very positive and encouraging words. Think especially about how they connect faith with joyful praise. And sometimes it's not so obvious. You may have never noticed the connections before, but they're there. I encourage you to find and enjoy them.

An Overflow of Joy

I urge you to use each one of these passages as a stimulus to joy and praise. As an overflow of gladness in your heart, write down your praise for Jesus in response to each verse.

O you who love the LORD, hate evil! He preserves the lives of his saints; he delivers them from the hand of the wicked. Light is sown for the righteous, and joy for the upright in heart. Rejoice in the LORD, O you righteous, and give thanks to his holy name! (Psalm 97:10-12)—

Glad songs of salvation are in the tents of the righteous: "The right hand of the LORD does valiantly, the right hand of the LORD exalts, the right hand of the LORD does valiantly!" I shall not die, but I shall live, and recount the deeds of the LORD. The LORD has disciplined me severely, but he has not given me over to death (Psalm 118:15-18)—

I will praise the LORD as long as I live; I will sing praises to my God while I have my being (Psalm 146:2)—

[Jesus said,] "So also you have sorrow now, but I will see you again, and your hearts will rejoice, and no one will take your joy from you" (John 16:22)—

Therefore, since we have been justified by faith, we have peace with God through our Lord Jesus Christ. Through him we have also obtained access by faith into this grace in which we stand, and we rejoice in hope of the glory of God. More than that, we rejoice in our sufferings, knowing that suffering produces endurance, and endurance produces character, and character produces hope, and hope does not put us to shame, because God's love has been poured into our hearts through the Holy Spirit who has been given to us (Romans 5:1-5)—

Neither death nor life, nor angels nor rulers, nor things present nor things to come, nor powers, nor height nor depth, nor anything else in all creation, will be able to separate us from the love of God in Christ Jesus our Lord (Romans 8:38-39)—

May the God of hope fill you with all joy and peace in believing, so that by the power of the Holy Spirit you may abound in hope (Romans 15:13)—

Rejoicing in Suffering

True faith discovers how to rejoice even in sufferings. That's difficult to comprehend, isn't it. Let's take a look at some passages that will help us grow in this area.

What Are Your Thoughts?

✤ After each passage, write down your thoughts and then share them with God, being honest about your beliefs and any hesitations or questions you may have.

[Jesus said,] "Blessed are you when others revile you and persecute you and utter all kinds of evil against you falsely on my account. Rejoice and be glad, for your reward is great in heaven" (Matthew 5:11-12)—

More than that, we rejoice in our sufferings, knowing that suffering produces endurance, and endurance produces character, and character produces hope, and hope does not put us to shame, because God's love has been poured into our hearts through the Holy Spirit who has been given to us (Romans 5:3-5)—

Blessed be the God and Father of our Lord Jesus Christ, the Father of mercies and God of all comfort, who comforts us in all our affliction, so that we may be able to comfort those who are in any affliction, with the comfort with which we ourselves are comforted by God. For as we share abundantly in Christ's sufferings, so through Christ we share abundantly in comfort too (2 Corinthians 1:3-5)—

Whatever gain I had, I counted as loss for the sake of Christ. Indeed, I count everything as loss because of the surpassing worth of knowing Christ Jesus my Lord. For his sake I have suffered the loss of all things and count them as rubbish, in order that I may gain Christ and be found in him, not having a righteousness of my own that comes from the law, but that which comes through faith in Christ, the righteousness from God that depends on

faith—that I may know him and the power of his resurrection, and may share his sufferings, becoming like him
in his death, that by any means possible I may attain the
resurrection from the dead (Philippians 3:7-11)—

Beloved, do not be surprised at the fiery trial when it
comes upon you to test you, as though something strange
were happening to you. But rejoice insofar as you share
Christ's sufferings, that you may also rejoice and be glad
when his glory is revealed (1 Peter 4:12-13)—

Those who sow in tears shall reap with shouts of joy!
(Psalm 126:5)—

❀ Why does it take *faith* to rejoice in suffering?

❀ When you undergo suffering, what are the most important truths
you can remember about God and yourself to help you rejoice during afflictions?

❀ Is suffering something you have learned to embrace? Why or why
not?

Deep Waters

In an earlier chapter I mentioned Charles Spurgeon's devotional book *Faith's Checkbook,* which is all about the promises of God. In the preface, Spurgeon gives some indication of some of the afflictions in his life during the time he was writing the book:

> I was wading in the surf of controversy. Since then I have been cast into "waters to swim in," which, but for God's upholding hand, would have proved waters to drown in.
>
> I have endured tribulation from many flails. Sharp bodily pain succeeded mental depression, and this was accompanied both by bereavement, and affliction in the person of one dear as life. The waters rolled in continually, wave upon wave. I do not mention this to exact sympathy, but simply to let the reader see that I am no dry-land sailor. I have traversed full many a time those oceans which are not Pacific: I know the roll of the billows, and the rush of the winds. Never were the promises of Jehovah so precious to me as at this hour. Some of them I never understood till now; I had not reached the date at which they matured, for I was not myself mature enough to perceive their meaning.
>
> How much more wonderful is the Bible to me now than it was a few months ago! In obeying the Lord, and bearing His reproach outside the camp, I have not received new promises; but the result to me is much the same as if I had done so, for the old ones have opened up to me with richer stores. Specially has the Word of the Lord to His servant Jeremiah sounded exceedingly sweet in mine ears. His lot it was to speak to those who would not hear, or hearing, would not believe. His was the sorrow which comes of disappointed love, and resolute loyalty; he would have turned his people from their errors, but he would not himself quit the way of the Lord. For him

there were words of deep sustaining power, which kept his mind from failing where nature unaided must have sunk. These and such like golden sentences of grace I have loved more than my necessary food, and with them I have enriched these pages.

Oh, that I might comfort some of my Master's servants! I have written out of my own heart with the view of comforting their hearts. I would say to them in their trials— My brethren, God is good. He will not forsake you: He will bear you through. There is a promise prepared for your present emergencies; and if you will believe and plead it at the mercy-seat through Jesus Christ, you shall see the hand of the Lord stretched out to help you. Everything else will fail, but His word never will. He has been to me so faithful in countless instances that I must encourage you to trust Him. I should be ungrateful to God and unkind to you if I did not do so.

May the Holy Spirit, the Comforter, inspire the people of the Lord with fresh faith! I know that, without His divine power, all that I can say will be of no avail; but, under His quickening influence, even the humblest testimony will confirm feeble knees, and strengthen weak hands. God is glorified when His servants trust Him implicitly. We cannot be too much of children with our heavenly Father. Our young ones ask no question about our will or our power, but having once received a promise from father, they rejoice in the prospect of its fulfillment, never doubting that it is sure as the sun...

May our Lord Jesus accept this my service for His sheep and lambs, from His unworthy Servant,

C.H. Spurgeon

Finding Joy in God's Promises

What Are Your Thoughts?

🎕 When you face severe suffering, why is it so important to keep the clearest view possible of God's promises?

God, I'm Ready to Walk in Faith has taken us through a great many of God's promises. All the promises of God are like food or fuel for our faith.

As we near the end of our time together, let me offer you just a few more of God's wonderful promises from his Good Book for you to reflect on and cherish. Some of these will be familiar, but I encourage you to receive each one with fresh new eyes and an open heart.

What Are Your Thoughts?

🎕 After each of the following passages, write down what you most appreciate about them. Also note what the personal message to you is in each one.

> If my people who are called by my name humble themselves, and pray and seek my face and turn from their wicked ways, then I will hear from heaven and will forgive their sin and heal their land (2 Chronicles 7:14)—

> The LORD is merciful and gracious, slow to anger and abounding in steadfast love. He will not always chide, nor will he keep his anger forever. He does not deal with us according to our sins, nor repay us according to our iniquities. For as high as the heavens are above the earth, so great is his steadfast love toward those who fear him;

as far as the east is from the west, so far does he remove our transgressions from us (Psalm 103:8-12)—

The LORD your God is in your midst, a mighty one who will save; he will rejoice over you with gladness; he will quiet you by his love; he will exult over you with loud singing (Zephaniah 3:17)—

[Jesus said,] "Everyone who acknowledges me before men, I also will acknowledge before my Father who is in heaven" (Matthew 10:32)—

[Jesus said,] "If anyone serves me, he must follow me; and where I am, there will my servant be also. If anyone serves me, the Father will honor him" (John 12:26)—

[Jesus said,] "You will receive power when the Holy Spirit has come upon you, and you will be my witnesses in Jerusalem and in all Judea and Samaria, and to the end of the earth" (Acts 1:8)—

For the Lord himself will descend from heaven with a cry of command, with the voice of an archangel, and with the sound of the trumpet of God. And the dead in Christ will rise first. Then we who are alive, who are left, will be caught up together with them in the clouds to meet the Lord in the air, and so we will always be with the Lord (1 Thessalonians 4:16-17)—

Walking by Faith

As we consider one final question, reflect on these words from Paul: "For we walk by faith, not by sight" (2 Corinthians 5:7).

What Are Your Thoughts?

✿ In light of everything you've learned in our study together about faith, what does walking by faith not by sight mean to you?

God, I'm Ready to Walk in Faith
Seminar DVD

Popular speaker and author
Thelma "Mama T" Wells
tells it like it is in the struggle to trust God

❧

Walk in faith? Maybe you feel it's all you can do just to walk the next step. Mama T can help! In six 30-minute sessions, she lays it on the line. In this dynamic seminar she shares how she overcame her struggles with believing and trusting God. Through Scripture she reveals how you can get your heart ready for God's gifts of success, contentment, purpose—and much more—by…

- submitting your life, goals, and dreams to Him
- praying about the goals and visions He gives you and waiting with patience
- weeding out the enemies of faith and making room for His abundance
- learning more about who He is and what He's like
- taking the faith risk of trusting in His generous, gracious plans for you

In life's hard things and not-so-hard things, Mama T will inspire you to step out in reliance on God and step forward with new hope, joy, and direction!

Six 30-minute sessions
Great for small groups, Bible studies, and church settings

About Thelma

THELMA WELLS' life has been a courageous journey of faith. Born to an unwed and physically disabled teenager, the name on Thelma's birth certificate read simply "Baby Girl Morris." Her mother worked as a maid in the "big house" while they lived in the servants' quarters. When Thelma stayed at her grandparents' home, her mentally ill grandmother locked her in a dark, smelly, insect-infested closet all day. To ease her fear, Thelma sang every hymn and praise song she knew.

A trailblazer for black women, Thelma worked in the banking industry and was a professor at Master's International School of Divinity. Her vivacious personality and talent for storytelling attracted the attention of the Women of Faith Tour. She was soon one of their core speakers. She was named Extraordinary Woman of the Year in 2008 by the Extraordinary Women Conferences. She also received the Advanced Writers and Speakers Association's Lifetime Achievement Award in 2009.

Along with writing books, including *Don't Give In...God Wants You to Win!* Thelma is president of Woman of God Ministries. "Mama T," as she is affectionately called, helps girls and women all over the world discover Jesus and live for Him.

Thelma earned degrees at North Texas State University and Master's International School of Divinity. She was awarded an honorary Ph.D. from St. Thomas Christian College and Theological Seminary and ordained through the Association of Christian Churches in Florida.

Thelma and George, her husband of 48 years, enjoy spending time with their children, grandchildren, and great-grandchildren.

For more information about Thelma and her ministry, check out

www.thelmawells.com

God Calls You "Winner"!

Is stress, indecision, heartache, or fear zapping your energy? Popular speaker and author Thelma Wells says life doesn't have to be that way! Opening her heart and God's Word, she reveals how God taught her to stand tall to win against discouragement and oppression by putting on God's armor. You'll discover...

- what spiritual warfare is
- who you're fighting
- what you're accomplishing

No human wins every fight, so Thelma encourages you to call on Jesus when you get tired. He wants you to win, and He actively participates with you to ensure victory.

Don't Give In...God Wants You to Win! DVD

Want a more personal experience with Mama T? Join an enthusiastic Texas audience and learn from her down-to-earth Bible teaching how to keep your joy, hold on to your hopes and dreams, and get closer to the only Person who can *guarantee* winning strategies in life. *2 DVDs, 2 sessions, total running time 112 minutes*

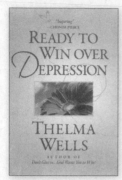

Ready to Win™ over Depression

Has sadness has taken over? Are you slogging through your day? Sharing personal stories and God's wisdom, Thelma "Mama T" Wells takes you on an easy-to-read journey out of depression. Through interactive questions you'll explore where you're at, and then discover practical suggestions for countering negativity, including discovering why God loves you and understanding how Jesus can help.

Ready to Win™ over Worry and Anxiety

Are you anxious about your family, job, health, or finances? Offering hope and compassion, Thelma helps you evaluate your worries, offers biblical wisdom to give you strength, and provides doable steps to kick anxiety out of your life. Together you will explore the impact of worry in your life and find out how your faith in God will see you through this time of turmoil.

Mama T Says, "Rise and Shine"

It's a brand-new day! Dynamic, upbeat, and forthright, "Mama T" encourages you to choose joy every day…and explains how to do that. Through powerful stories that highlight God's amazing presence, love, wisdom, and provision, Mama T shows you how to draw closer to Jesus, experience the help He offers, and put joy and contentment into your day.